Pot It Up

Pot It Up

150 Fresh Ideas for Beautiful, Easy-to-Grow Containers

FRANKIE FLOWERS

PHOTOGRAPHY BY
SHANNON J. ROSS

Collins

Published by Collins, an imprint of HarperCollins Publishers Ltd.

First Edition

HarperCollins books may be purchased for educational, business
or sales promotional use through our Special Markets Department.

HarperCollins Publishers Ltd.
2 Bloor Street East, 20th Floor
Toronto, Ontario, Canada
M4W 1A8

www.harpercollins.ca

Library and Archives Canada Cataloguing in Publication

Flowers, Frankie
Pot it up : 150 fresh ideas for beautiful, easy-to-grow containers/
Frankie Flowers ; photography by Shannon J. Ross.

ISBN 978-1-55468-834-0

1. Container gardening. 2. Plants, Potted. I. Ross, Shannon J II. Title.

SB418.F55 2012   635.9'86   C2011-905715-8

Printed and bound in Canada
TC 9 8 7 6 5 4 3 2 1

To my wife, Laurie.
A spouse is a partner in life who supports your roots
and lets you bloom to your potential.
I love you!

CONTENTS

Pot It Up

Intro

I love container gardening, and I'm not the only one: its popularity has grown immensely over the last decade. In many parts of the country, property sizes have decreased and more home-owners are finding themselves in condos with no garden space at all. Many others are just looking for a simple way to add immediate impact to a porch, patio, or front entrance. *The whole world is going to pot!* My goal in *Pot It Up* is to show you how to create containers that will be the talk of the town.

I like to think of containers as though they were paintings. So I'll first show you how to select the right pot, which is the frame around your picture: it helps complement the artwork inside it. I'll explain how to use the right soil, which is like the canvas. Then comes the fun part: choosing the plants that add the colour and texture to your work of art. I'll show you a gallery of 150 plant combinations for different seasons and different tastes.

I've tried to give you a lot of guidance in these pages, but you don't need to follow my examples to the letter—just use them as a guide to create your own mixes. Like all great artists, you shouldn't be afraid to experiment. Some plants will eventually die (it happens to all of us), but some of the best mixes come out of trial and error. Although this book is full of gorgeous plant combinations, the truth is that some of my experiments didn't make it into these pages. Some just didn't perform; others grew well but resembled the bad shirts at the back of my closet.

Why Containers?

Containers turn dull spaces into interesting places. Just take an empty pot, add a few plants, and presto! Here are a few reasons why you should consider container gardening:

They grow where traditional gardens don't

The main advantage of containers is that they can grow just about anywhere. They're an ideal way to add beauty and colour to a condo terrace, a walkway, or the entrance to a townhouse. You can even use containers in a traditional garden—they can become colourful focal points and are often great replacements for specimen trees or shrubs in areas where these larger plants just don't have enough space to grow. Have a spot in the garden with a tree stump or poor soil? No problem: fill it with a container.

They offer quick fixes

A well-planned garden has something to offer in every season, from early spring blooms to vibrant fall colours. But these changes come slowly and gradually. With a container, you get results right away. In fact, I change my containers every season to instantly create a little conversation, or to add some drama to my garden, patio, or entrance. Containers can be moved, changed, and replanted easily to update the look of your home.

They go exactly where you need them

My wife is a realtor, and I've helped her improve some less-than-desirable properties with container gardens. I'll use them in front of an air conditioner or hydro meter to draw attention to the plants instead of the eyesore.

At home, I have several pots of herbs right outside my kitchen, close to the barbecue, so I have easy access and can make quick adjustments to the flavour of whatever I'm preparing.

They're easy on the body

Gardening can be hard on the back and knees. People with mobility issues often love container gardening because they don't have to bend over as far to reach the plants and less weeding is required.

They rein in invasive plants

Sometimes what containers do best is *contain*. Mint, for example, is a useful and easy-to-grow herb, but if you plant it in the garden, it will take over. When placed inside a pot, its roots are contained, so it can't spread.

A well-designed container can add colour and texture to your entranceway, deck, poolside, or backyard patio. Containers are also an excellent introduction for novices who want to experiment with planting before investing in a full-size garden.

They allow you to grow tropicals

You love hibiscus, bougainvillea, passion flowers, palms, oleander, and cactus—but you live in Canada. No problem: containers allow you to accessorize your poolside and patio with a whole range of tropical plants with a Caribbean feel. And, with the threat of Jack Frost in the fall, you can easily bring the containers indoors.

The Challenges

For new property owners and novice gardeners, containers are an excellent introduction to plants, design, and garden maintenance in a small, manageable format. But they do bring their own challenges.

They need a lot of water

Plants in containers dry out quickly because of the lack of soil mass and because the root balls are more exposed to sun and wind than if planted in the ground. A property with many pots of plants can be more maintenance than a garden filled with water-wise or native plants.

They need to be fertilized regularly

Container soil lacks the natural nutrients found in regular garden soil (more about this later). Frequent watering also tends to wash away the small amount of nutrients that *are* present. That means you'll need to fertilize your containers regularly to supply the nutrients your plants need to grow and bloom.

Even perennials may not survive

Depending on where you live, most perennials will die if you leave them outdoors in a container over the winter. A pot just doesn't provide enough insulation, and the roots will freeze. If you want your perennials to survive until the next spring, you'll need to remove them from the pot and plant them in the garden before the frost arrives.

You have to store them in winter

Pots made of clay, concrete, or plastic may break if the soil and moisture in them freezes and expands. They'll need to be emptied and stored for the winter, so even when they're not in use they'll take up space.

They're not cheap

A 40 cm (16-inch) container—the size we use for this book—including the pot, the soil, and the plants, will cost about $50 on average. You can get that down to about $20 if you use a plastic pot and common annuals, but if you use more exotic plants, that price tag can easily climb above $100. If you're updating your containers every season, that can really add up. You can get better value by using perennials, which you can move to the garden after enjoying them in the container. I'll tell you exactly how to do this in the pages that follow.

Although you can keep your costs down by using common plant varieties and plastic pots, container gardening can get expensive: expect to pay about $50 on average. Pots can also require a lot of water, so keep a watering can or hose nearby.

Pot It Up

Container Basics

Understanding your location

There are many factors that go into your choice of plants for a container garden, but the most important is the pot's location.

If you're placing a container in a windy location, for example, avoid using tall plants with large leaves; these will just get torn up, and the whole container could topple. Wind also dries out containers quickly, so you'll want to use drought-tolerant plants. If your pot will be in a high-traffic area—where it will contend with kids and crazy drunken neighbours—choose rough-and-tumble plants that will bounce back if they take a beating.

The amount of light the container receives is critical when choosing plants. Here's a guide to help:

Selecting your container

Have you ever noticed how different someone looks when they change clothes? The same person can look elegant, rugged, scruffy, or refined depending on what he or she is wearing. The same is true for containers: although the plants inside may be the same, the packaging can't be ignored. Your choice of container can have a dramatic effect on the overall look of your space.

For the combinations in this book, we used the simplest pot around: a standard 40 cm (16-inch) plastic container that you can find at any garden centre for about $10. When adapting these ideas for your home, however, choose a container that suits your property and your individual tastes.

When choosing a container, consider the following factors:

Location. Is the area windy? If so, a heavy container such as one made of concrete or metal will ensure your plants don't end up spilled all over the ground. If you're placing the container near the driveway, look for one that can survive the odd tussle with a bicycle.

Style. What kind of look do you want to achieve? If Mediterranean is your style, then clay or stone are good choices. (Be warned: clay pots look great, but they break easily when they freeze. Consider plastic or fibreglass pots that have the look of clay but are more durable.) For a modern look, consider using plastic, metal, or fibreglass with slick edges. A glossy finish really complements Asian-inspired combinations. To get a country look, I like to go to antique stores and look for old steel tubs or jugs.

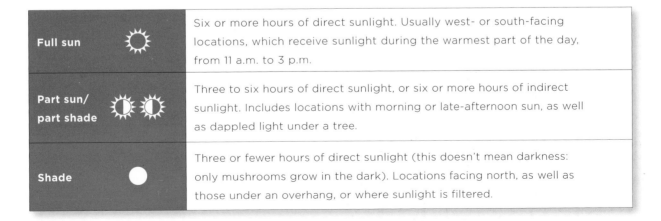

Full sun	☀	Six or more hours of direct sunlight. Usually west- or south-facing locations, which receive sunlight during the warmest part of the day, from 11 a.m. to 3 p.m.
Part sun/ part shade	◐ ◑	Three to six hours of direct sunlight, or six or more hours of indirect sunlight. Includes locations with morning or late-afternoon sun, as well as dappled light under a tree.
Shade	●	Three or fewer hours of direct sunlight (this doesn't mean darkness: only mushrooms grow in the dark). Locations facing north, as well as those under an overhang, or where sunlight is filtered.

Pretty much anything that can hold potting soil will work as a container: watering cans, saucepans, bathtubs, the kitchen sink, old boots. But in the world of traditional container gardening, there are some mainstays:

Type	Uses	Pros	Cons
Clay (terracotta)	Traditional gardens, Italian gardens, for growing cactuses	Porous, which helps promote root health and reduces risk of over-watering	Heavy, easily broken, and not frost resistant; tend to dry out faster; limited colour range
Plastic	Anywhere and everywhere	Inexpensive, durable, lightweight, available in every colour	Easily blown over, not frost resistant, non-porous
Metal	High-traffic areas	Non-breakable, durable	Heavy, expensive
Stone/concrete	Windy areas	Stable, natural looking	Heavy, not frost resistant, expensive
Fibreglass	As a substitute for concrete	Lightweight but durable, natural-looking, frost resistant	Expensive
Rice/corn/fibre	As "grower pots" for seedlings	Recyclable, environmentally friendly	Last for only a short period before breaking down

Size. Make sure the pot is adequate for the plants that you want to grow and suited to its location. The container should not dominate or look lost in your space. (If you have a grand entranceway, you don't want a small white hanging basket.) In general, I would rather have fewer large containers than a whole bunch of small ones. Plants always do better in larger pots, and the extra soil mass will give you more time in between watering and fertilizing.

Storage space. Many pots need to be emptied and stored for the winter. Do you have the space? If not, select pots that are frost resistant. Ask the garden centre staff when you purchase your container; many new designs (particularly plastic ones) are double-walled and can tolerate being outdoors all year long.

Prepping your pot

After you've selected the right pot for your setting, you may need to make some adjustments.

Drainage is especially important in container gardening. Have you ever sat in a tub of water for 24 hours? Well, your plants don't want to either. Overwatering and lack of drainage lead to root rot, which can cause a potted plant's demise. So make sure your container has good drainage holes. (If you plan to bring your container indoors for the winter and are worried about having the plant damage your windowsill or table, you can also place a tray underneath to catch any overflow.)

My grandfather always said that the best way to create drainage in a container is to drill several holes in the bottom. The number and size depend on the pot. For example, with a 25 cm (10-inch) pot, five 2 cm (3/4-inch) holes will do the trick. Drainage holes allow water and air to flow in and out freely, keeping the roots and the rest of the plant healthy.

However, with some materials, such as clay or metal, drilling holes is not an option. In that case, you'll need to place something coarse in the bottom third of the pot to allow for drainage. Crushed gravel, stones, broken clay pots, or even plastic water bottles can be used. (Some people recommend using Styrofoam packing peanuts. This sounds like a good idea until you need to empty your containers on a windy day in the fall and bits of Styrofoam end up all over your property.) Always ensure the material will not adjust the acidity (or pH) of the soil. Limestone gravel, for example, will decrease the acidity.

Pots come in all sizes and materials, and choosing the right one depends on your location and personal taste. In general, select the largest pot that your space can comfortably accommodate. Plants always do better when they have plenty of room to grow.

Frost Resistant Versus Frost Tolerant

You'll see throughout the book that I sometimes refer to plants or materials as either frost resistant or frost tolerant. *Frost resistant* describes pots or plants that are ready and able to take on the coldest winter temperatures. They're happy to be left outdoors all year long. *Frost tolerant*, on the other hand, refers to those cold-hardy plants that can withstand a light frost but not a deep freeze (anything below –5°C/23°F and they're done). Look for these terms to help guide your cold-season plant and materials choices.

Keeping your pots off the ground even by 2.5 cm (1 inch) is another way to improve drainage and increase airflow to the roots, maintaining the overall health of your plants. You can buy pot "feet" at the garden centre, or you can make your own using wood wedges or broken brick—anything that will lift the container just that little bit off the ground.

Here's another tip: if your container has large drainage holes, lay coffee filters over the holes before adding the soil. These will prevent the soil from escaping through the holes but will still allow water to flow through.

For windy spaces, use a material that will add weight to the pot, such as stones. If you expect to be moving your pots frequently, choose something lighter, such as water bottles. A sheet of landscape fabric laid over the drainage material can help keep the soil from settling and will still allow water to seep through.

Using the right soil

Let's make one thing clear right now: garden soil, manure, triple mix, and topsoil are not meant to be used in containers. These types of soil and amendments are too heavy, they dry out quickly, and they don't allow the flow of oxygen to the roots.

When you're gardening with containers, you need to use a growing medium designed specifically for the job. They're called "soilless" mixes because they don't contain much organic material. There are two popular types:

Container soil is a blend of peat moss and humus with an added combination of sand, calcined clay, and organic fertilizer. The sand improves drainage when you overwater and during prolonged periods of wet weather, and the calcined clay increases moisture retention during dry spells.

Good drainage is essential for healthy containers. Most plastic pots have holes in the bottom, but to improve drainage further, you can place some bulky items in the container before adding the soil. Smaller pots, plastic water bottles, or stones will do the trick.

Regular garden soil is not suitable for containers! Instead, select a high-quality potting soil or container soil. These are made up primarily of peat moss and humus, with other materials designed to prevent soil compaction and retain moisture.

Potting soil is also a blend of peat moss and humus (some include organic fertilizer), but instead of sand and clay, it includes vermiculite and perlite. These minerals are designed to retain moisture and prevent soil compaction. Potting soil is ideal for tropicals like palms, peace lilies, and yucca, and it can be used for houseplants as well as outdoors.

The range of choices of containers and potting mixes are endless. Most offer little more than marketing hype, though some really do retain moisture for very long periods—they seem to hold liquid like a baby's diaper. Although these do help plants survive during prolonged drought, they may be counterproductive during periods of wet weather, when the roots could rot. I prefer to avoid them and just develop good watering habits.

You could make your own container soil, and as greenhouse growers my family used to do that. But now I recommend purchasing it by the bag. Price usually determines quality, and you get what you pay for.

In some cases, you can add traditional garden soil or amendments to potting soil to create a balanced mix. For example, if your large containers are drying out too fast, adding one-quarter topsoil or triple mix to the existing potting soil can help. This will reduce moisture loss and at the same time will add some nutrients to the pot.

I'm often asked whether container soil can be used year after year. With small containers, the answer is usually no. To reduce the risk of disease, I recommend starting with new soil. For large containers—anything larger than 30 cm (12 inches)—you can get away with freshening up only the top third of the soil. However, if your plants experienced disease or struggled last season, the answer is easy: start with new soil this year after cleaning the pots with a weak bleach solution (a capful of bleach to 1 litre/4 cups of water).

Choosing a Design

In this book, I'll give you 150 of my design ideas, but I want you to feel free to experiment with your own plant mixes. I know this can be intimidating for a new gardener, so here are some tips that can help. Containers are mini-landscapes, and your goal is to make them interesting by combining different textures, colours, and heights. Whenever I plant a container, I remember the phrase "thriller, filler, spiller."

Thrillers provide the drama in a container. They're typically the tallest element in the mix—anything from the good old dracaena spike, to Canna lilies, to ornamental grasses, or even vine-type plants on a trellis, such as scarlet runner beans. Thrillers don't even have to be plants—a statue, or cut stems of forsythia in early spring, can give your container the thrill it needs.

As a general rule, I recommend using only one thriller (or one grouping) in a container. I also suggest that it should not be more than twice the height of your container. Thrillers should be placed near the middle or toward the rear of the container. You want the thriller to draw the eye but, at the same time, you don't want it to restrict light to the other plants.

Fillers are the plants that give body and substance to a container by surrounding the thriller. Popular filler plants include coleus, sedum, geraniums, and coral bells—any plant that will not dominate and does not trail. They can be perennials, annuals, herbs, or tropicals. I recommend one filler in a 25 cm (10-inch) pot, and one to three in a 40 cm (16-inch) container.

Spillers create flow by pouring over the edge of a container, like water from an overfilled bathtub. 'Wave' petunias, German ivy, potato vine, ivy geraniums, vinca vine, creeping Jenny, and even oregano are all examples of spillers. I always recommend keeping things simple when it comes to spillers. One or two types are almost always enough.

There are exceptions to the "thrill, fill, spill" rule. I've seen some containers make a dramatic impact with only one type of plant, especially when grouped with other planters with similar colours or styles. Never ignore the fact that some plants just look great alone.

Good design combines texture, colour and height. A simple rule of thumb is to include three main elements: a "thriller" to provide height and drama, a "filler" to add substance, and a "spiller" to trail over the pot's edge and create flow. See page 65 for instructions on how to plant this container.

Frankie's Favourite Thrillers

Plant	Light requirements	Fantastic feature	Season
Canna	Full sun	Large tropical leaves in a wide range of colours, plus fabulous flowers on spiky stems.	Summer
Colocasia	Part sun	Nicknamed "elephant ears" for its huge leaves, which add drama with their dark colours.	Summer
Cut stems	Any	Unique shapes and colours add instant interest with zero mainte-nance, even in winter. Best bets include dogwood, pussy willow, curly willow, forsythia, crabapple, and magnolia.	Spring/Fall/Winter
Hibiscus	Full sun	An easy way to recreate the tropics in your containers. Glossy green leaves and bright single or double blooms in shades of red, yellow, pink, and peach.	Summer
Ornamental grasses	Full to part sun, depending on variety	Lots of variety in size, blade colour, and moisture requirements, including some that are drought tolerant. Complement other plant-ings and look great on their own.	Summer

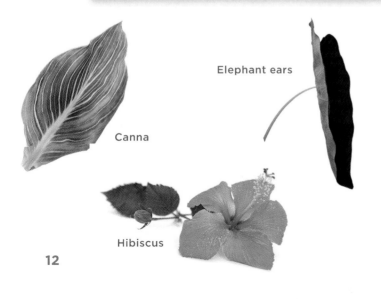

Canna

Elephant ears

Hibiscus

Pussy willow
(stems)

Pink
fountain grass

Pot It Up

Frankie's Favourite Fillers

Plant	Light requirements	Fantastic feature	Season
Coleus	Full sun to shade, depending on variety	An enormous number of varieties, many with fabulous multicoloured foliage. Very vigorous growers, even in shady spots.	Summer
'Dragon Wing' begonia	Full to part sun	A foolproof annual with large wax-like leaves combined with prolific flowers in shades of red and pink.	Summer
Heuchera (coral bells)	Part sun to shade	A versatile and varied family of perennials available in a wide range of leaf colours (red, burgundy, chartreuse, and more). Offers interest in a container throughout the season.	Spring/Summer/Fall
Impatiens	Part sun to shade	The easiest way to add sizzle all summer long. Constant blooms in red, white, purple, pink, orange, and lavender. Thrives in the shade.	Summer
Sedum (stonecrop)	Full sun	Upright varieties with lush, succulent foliage add interest all season and blooms in late summer or fall. Tough, drought tolerant, and thrives in poor soil.	Summer/Fall

Coleus

Heuchera
(coral bells)

Impatiens

Sedum

'Dragon Wing'
begonia

Frankie's Favourite Spillers

Plant	Light requirements	Fantastic feature	Season
Calibrachoa (million bells)	Full to part sun	A colourful trailing annual with tons of small trumpet-shaped flowers. Available in white, pink, orange, purple, red, and bicoloured varieties.	Summer/Fall
Sweet potato vine (ipomoea)	Full sun	Who needs flowers when you have such awesome foliage? A vigorous grower available in many leaf varieties (from heart-shaped to finger-shaped) and a range of colours, from lime to rust to black.	Summer
Torenia	Part sun to shade	A shade-loving annual with a trailing form and wonderful blooms in white and blue.	Summer
Trailing verbena	Full sun	Easy-to-grow annual with bright blooms in pink, orange, red, and purple. Just be sure to look for mildew-resistant varieties.	Summer
'Wave' petunia	Full to part sun	Among the world's bestselling annuals because it's an amazing performer and needs almost no maintenance. Available with single and double blooms in red, white, blue, pink, and (my favourite) purple.	Summer

Calibrachoa

Sweet potato vine

Torenia

Trailing verbena

'Wave' petunia

Pot It Up

Choosing Colours

When designing your container, don't make the common mistake of using too many colours. I like to stick to just one to three colours. (I have seen containers work well with five or more, but usually they look like the dog's breakfast.) Here are some tips:

Monochromatic containers combine several plant varieties with one central colour. The colour may be different shades and strengths, and the plants should have different growth habits and textures. These harmonies are quiet and soothing.

Consider combining plants whose colours are **analogous,** or closely related. These appear beside each other on the colour wheel, such as red, orange, and yellow, and add a dramatic flair. You might also use two analogous colours, such as pink and purple, in combination with white to create a calm look.

Complementary colours are widely spaced on the colour wheel. For example, you might combine yellow daffodils and blue grape hyacinths. These are standout combinations that often create energy and excitement.

Neutral colours (black, grey, and white) may not be on the colour wheel, but they do have a place in your pots. White helps reflect light in dull corners, while grey and dark-leafed plants add depth. Plants with grey or dark foliage make an excellent backdrop, allowing other plantings to stand out. Both look great in combination with white.

In coming up with container designs, try to think in terms of a theme. Surrounding my pool, for example, I use a theme I call "tropical punch." It includes plants of different heights, growing habits, and textures, with blooms of orange and purple, such as hibiscus, Canna lilies, million bells, gerbera daisies, zinnias, and 'Wave' petunias. To keep with the tropical theme, some of my containers use palms as the thrillers.

The time of year will not only determine your plant selections but also help shape the theme. Entrance containers should always be planted with seasonality in mind: they'll keep your home looking current. Spring containers might include twigs of pussy willow (the thriller), underplanted with yellow tulips and blue pansies (the fillers), and yellow violas spilling over the edge. Fall containers may have corn-like millet as the thriller, underplanted with chrysanthemums, ornamental cabbage, or kale, with trailing ivy.

Often you can update your container simply by removing tired-looking plants and replacing them with plants that scream the season. Pansies look cheerful in the spring, but by early summer they're past their best-before date. Replace them with begonias or geraniums, which will last until frost.

Buying Your Plants

Chances are you'll be raring to get into the garden centre in spring so you can fill the trunk of your car with container plants. But before you head out, figure out how many plants you will need. This depends, of course, on the size of the container and whether you're using plants grown in individual 5 cm (2-inch) cells or larger varieties that come in 10 cm (4-inch) pots. For example, a 25 cm (10-inch) container will require five cells or three 10 cm (4-inch) pots. You can use larger plants to create instant gratification, but the key is to not overplant the container. Use this guide to help you plan:

Avoid tall and leggy plants in favour of those with strong, stocky stems.

Examine the top and the underside of foliage for chew marks, discoloration, mould, or browning, all of which are signs of insects or disease.

A broken pot or container may indicate that the plant was dropped, and the root system may be damaged.

If you're used to buying plants for your garden, you probably understand hardiness zones. If not, here's a refresher: Canada is divided into nine zones, with 0 being the harshest (think arctic) and 8 being the mildest (a few areas of coastal B.C.). Hardiness zones take into account seasonal weather patterns like average minimum and maximum temperatures, number of

A PLANT PURCHASING GUIDE

Size of container	Number of 5 cm (2-inch) cells needed	Number of 10 cm (4-inch) pots needed
25 cm (10 inch)	5	3
30 cm (12 inch)	7	5
40 cm (16 inch)	11	9
50 cm (20 inch)	12	9
60 cm (24 inch)	15	11

Once you're at the garden centre, take the time to carefully examine each plant before purchasing.

Overall, you're looking for plants that appear vibrant—like they're just waiting to burst forth. The foliage should be lush, with deep colour.

Also look for lots of unopened buds, not plants that are already in full bloom.

Carefully lift the plant out of its pot and look for roots that are white and firm, not dark and soft or rotten. Also be wary of roots that are growing out of the container, which may indicate an older plant that will have difficulty getting established in a new location.

frost-free days, snow cover, and winds, as well as historical plant survival data. The idea is to let you know which plants are likely to overwinter in your garden. A plant that is hardy to Zone 5 will survive in Niagara Falls (Zone 6), but not in Edmonton (Zone 3). The lower the number, the colder the climate, and the number on a plant tag refers to the coldest zone a plant can tolerate. So, a plant with a Zone 4 tag cannot survive in a Zone 3 climate but will still thrive in a Zone 5 or Zone 6 climate.

In containers, these hardiness zones don't apply. During the winter, perennial plants in containers—

unlike those in a garden bed—are not insulated by snow and the warmth of the surrounding soil, so most will freeze and die. In my experience, you should expect a plant to overwinter in a container only if it is hardy to two zones colder than the one you live in. For example, if you live in Zone 5, look for plants hardy to Zone 3—or better yet, Zone 2.

As a rule, I don't recommend overwintering plants in pots. A few will make it through the ordeal—

I've had the best success with hosta and sedum. With others, you can try burying the whole pot in the garden and mounding soil around it. But with most of the containers described in this book, I'll tell you how and when to remove the perennials and transplant them in the garden to enjoy for years to come.

When selecting plants from the garden centre, look for lush, vibrant foliage and new buds that look ready to burst forth. Take a pass on plants that appear to be struggling, or whose blooms are already spent.

Plant Hardiness Zones of Canada

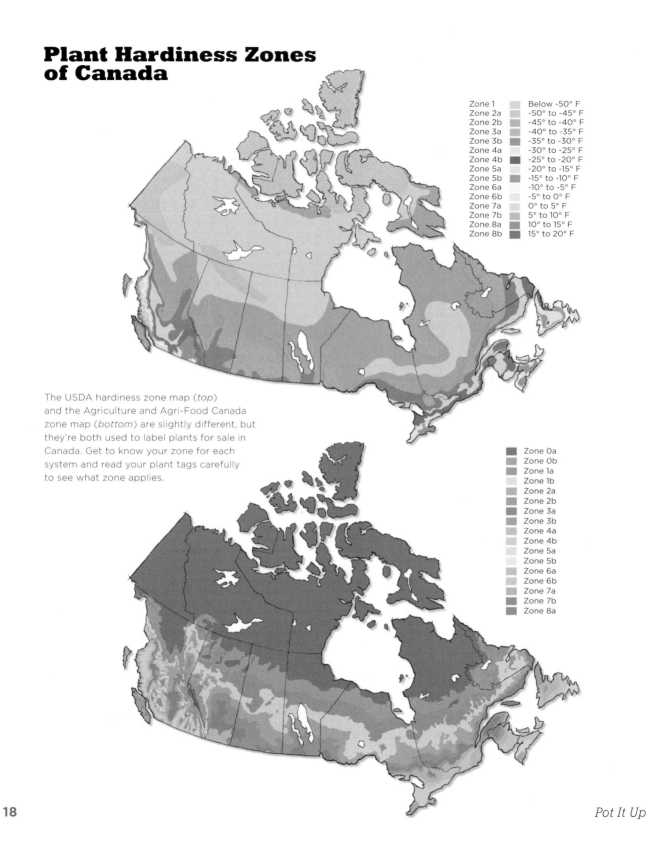

Zone 1	Below -50° F
Zone 2a	-50° to -45° F
Zone 2b	-45° to -40° F
Zone 3a	-40° to -35° F
Zone 3b	-35° to -30° F
Zone 4a	-30° to -25° F
Zone 4b	-25° to -20° F
Zone 5a	-20° to -15° F
Zone 5b	-15° to -10° F
Zone 6a	-10° to -5° F
Zone 6b	-5° to 0° F
Zone 7a	0° to 5° F
Zone 7b	5° to 10° F
Zone 8a	10° to 15° F
Zone 8b	15° to 20° F

The USDA hardiness zone map (*top*) and the Agriculture and Agri-Food Canada zone map (*bottom*) are slightly different, but they're both used to label plants for sale in Canada. Get to know your zone for each system and read your plant tags carefully to see what zone applies.

Zone 0a
Zone 0b
Zone 1a
Zone 1b
Zone 2a
Zone 2b
Zone 3a
Zone 3b
Zone 4a
Zone 4b
Zone 5a
Zone 5b
Zone 6a
Zone 6b
Zone 7a
Zone 7b
Zone 8a

Getting Down to Planting

Okay, time to get dirty! Gather all of your new plants and everything else you need to start planting:

- your container
- potting soil
- drainage supplement (such as broken clay pots or empty water bottles) if required, or a drill to make drainage holes in the container
- watering can
- trowel or large kitchen spoon
- garden gloves (optional but recommended)
- slow-release fertilizer (optional if you'll be fertilizing regularly during the growing season)
- pail or wheelbarrow to hold excess soil

Follow these steps:

1. Make sure your pot has adequate drainage. Drill holes or use another method if necessary (see page 7).
2. Fill the pot two-thirds full with container soil or potting soil.
3. Moisten soil thoroughly; you never want to plant in dry soil.
4. Start planting, beginning with the thriller at the centre or the back of the container. Plant the spiller close to the edge of the pot, and then add the fillers in the empty spaces. Unlike in a garden bed, you don't need to worry about the recommended spacing. Pack the plants in tightly so the container looks lush and full.
5. Top up the container with soil as necessary and pat down.
6. Water thoroughly.
7. Add the slow-release fertilizer if desired.
8. Place the container in the desired location.

Before planting, carefully slide each rootball out of its pot and loosen it with your fingers (*left*). Start at the back or the centre of the container and work toward the edges (*middle*), packing the plants in tightly but making sure you leave them some space to grow (*right*).

Keeping your containers looking great

There's really no such thing as a no-maintenance container garden. Keeping your pots looking vibrant and healthy takes a little effort.

Watering. The number one killer of container gardens is poor watering—either too much or too little. There is no simple formula for the right amount; it depends on the size of the container (small pots dry out faster), the location (sunny or windy spots require more frequent watering), and the type of plants (some enjoy being dry, while others need to be kept evenly moist). Plants that look wilted are usually telling you they need a drink, but be careful: sometimes a wilted plant can be a sign of overwatering.

The best way to determine if a container needs watering is to use the good old finger-touch method.

Water your containers thoroughly, making sure the moisture reaches the roots. If the water immediately drains out the bottom, repeat in a few minutes.

Just stick your finger about 2.5 cm (1 inch) into the soil. If it feels completely dry, it's time to water the container.

Unlike those in a garden bed, plants in containers can't draw water from a mass of soil surrounding them. And if you've placed your containers under an overhanging roof or other covered space, they won't receive any of Mother Nature's "tears of growth." I often remove the pots from my front porch during a rainfall and place them out in the open.

When watering containers, it's important to soak them thoroughly, making sure the moisture penetrates into the roots at the bottom of the pot. When pots are very dry, you may find that the water immediately runs out the bottom. If this happens, water the container thoroughly, wait five minutes, and repeat until the soilless mix expands and regains its ability to absorb moisture.

For smaller pots, I recommend filling a bucket or sink with water and sinking the pots up to the rim. As soon as the bubbles disappear, you can be sure your pot is fully watered.

Many pots need to be watered more than once a day in summer, making container gardening somewhat high maintenance. Never fear—technology is here! There are many irrigation systems, timers, and sensors designed for pots, as well as a number of soils on the market that have the ability to absorb moisture and release it slowly over time.

If you're going away for a long weekend in summer, remember to water your containers before you leave. It may also help to group them together and, if possible, place them in an area of indirect sunlight, sheltered from winds. If that's not an option, take a large plastic pop bottle and punch a few small holes near the mouth. Fill the bottle with water and place it upside down in the soil, deep enough that the surrounding soil will support it. As the soil dries out, water will slowly be released from the bottle.

Fertilizing. Because container and potting soils don't contain a lot of nutrients, you need to fertilize regularly to keep your plants looking vibrant. Most of the containers in this book should be fertilized every two weeks during the growing season. However, there are exceptions, and I've noted these in the individual Water description for each container.

When you look on the label of any fertilizer, you'll see three numbers, which are the N-P-K ratio. These tell you the amount of nitrogen, phosphorus, and potassium in the fertilizer. Nitrogen promotes green top growth; phosphorus encourages deep roots and vivid blooms; potassium helps guard against disease and makes plants more tolerant of drought and cold.

In general, three types of fertilizer are useful for containers:

20-20-20 is an all-purpose plant food. If you're not fussy and you want to buy just one fertilizer for all your containers, this is the one to get.

A fertilizer with a high middle number, such as 15-30-15, is perfect for flowering plants and those that produce fruit. If you want the brightest blooms and the biggest tomatoes, this is your fertilizer.

If you want your foliage containers to be lush and tropical-looking, look for a fertilizer with high nitrogen content, such as 30-12-12.

The ideal time to fertilize is immediately after a rain or right after watering. This opens up the soil and the roots so they can drink in the much-needed plant food.

Deadheading. No, it's not the name of a rock band. Deadheading refers to the removal of spent flowers to promote new growth, giving your containers more bloom for your buck. When you're deadheading, be sure to remove both the flower and stem, either by pinching with your fingernails or snipping with a pair of scissors.

To keep your containers blooming all season long, practise regular deadheading. By removing spent flowers and their stems, you're allowing the plant to redirect its energy toward new growth, as well as reducing the risk of disease.

All-purpose, water-soluble plant food is a good choice if you plan to fertilize throughout the season. If you want to feed your containers less often, add slow-release pellets when you plant.

Pot It Up

When your container is done for the season, plant the perennials in your garden. Remove the root ball and use a trowel or sharp knife to divide it. Prepare the garden bed by loosening the soil with a spade, and settle your transplanted shrub into its new home. If you want to plant this container, check out page 165.

Some annuals (such as impatiens and 'Wave' petunias) are labelled self-deadheading or self-cleaning, but in my experience you're best off doing it yourself. Many annuals will benefit from the removal of weak, leggy overgrowth. They'll come back stronger and more colourful.

In late July I'll often take a pair of scissors and cut back trailing petunias, lobelia, and potato vine. The results are always incredible: instead of my containers appearing tired near the season's end, they look fresh and fun.

Diseases and insects. Unfortunately, containers are not free from the diseases and insects that plague gardeners. Powdery mildew, black spot, aphids, and whiteflies are just a few of the problems you may encounter when container gardening.

The best way to avoid these problems is to purchase plants that are free of disease and insects to start with. Once you've planted your containers, however, make sure there is good airflow around the pot, as this will reduce the chance of disease. Try to keep water off the foliage and flowers: water only the base of the pot. Deadheading spent flowers will also prevent rot.

Inspect your containers thoroughly for insects. A spray of water will wash them away; a quick application of insecticidal soap will keep the more persistent ones at bay. Insecticidal soap, harmless to humans and pets, coats the shells of insects and suffocates them. You can make your own by mixing 5 mL (1 teaspoon) of dish soap with 1 litre (4 cups) of water. If some of your plants are struggling because of disease or insects, you're better off removing them and starting over—that way you both limit the chances they'll spread disease to other plants and reduce the amount of maintenance required. No needy plants need apply!

Closing Out the Growing Season

Although many of the plants recommended in this book are perennials, many will not survive winter in a container. However, you can enjoy these plants for many years if you remove them from the pot in late fall and plant them in the garden. If you want to recreate the same container in spring, you can dig up the perennial and plant it in the pot again.

"Parting out" your container means carefully removing the plants so you can separate the keepers from those that will end up in the compost. If it's a small 25 cm (10-inch) pot, you can just turn the container upside down to remove its contents, and then use a sharp knife to separate the plants. For a larger pot, dig each plant out individually with a trowel.

I'll have lots of suggestions to share in the Water descriptions of each individual container. But in general, you just need to make sure that you find a spot in the garden that has the right soil, light, and moisture conditions for your perennial. Save your plant tags, as they contain all this information.

Many tropical plants can be overwintered indoors in their containers—hibiscus, bougainvillea, oleander, and palms are just a few examples. They need to be taken inside in late summer or early fall, before the threat of frost.

Before you bring a plant indoors, I suggest spraying both the top and underside of the plant's leaves with insecticidal soap to reduce the risk of bringing bugs into your home. You may also do a light pruning at this time. Cut back about a third of the plant's overall growth to improve its shape, and remove any leggy, weak growth and dead or diseased stems.

Place the plant indoors in a brightly lit room; west- or south-facing windows are best. Ensure that the leaves are not touching the glass, and keep the

Insects such as beetles and aphids are a constant threat to your plants. A quick spray of homemade insecticidal soap will keep many six-legged pests at bay. Harmless to people and plants, the soap coats the shells of insects and suffocates them.

container away from vents or other heat sources, as these will stress and eventually kill the plants.

You may find a lot of leaf drop when you first bring your pots indoors. This is normal: plants need to adjust to their new environment. Hibiscus will sometimes totally lose their leaves, only to come back stronger. So don't make the mistake of thinking they need more water, as you may drown them.

As fall turns into winter, reduce your watering frequency, and from October through March use little or no fertilizer. In the spring, when daylight hours increase, your plants will start growing again, so you should start increasing the watering and fertilizing. Once the threat of frost has passed, you can slowly acclimatize the container to outdoor temperature and light levels. Just leave the container outside during the day and bring it in at night, and continue this for a week or two. I also suggest another light pruning at this time.

If you're leaving your containers outside over the winter, take special care to make sure they survive. Containers left upright will fill with water (even if there is soil left in them), and when this water freezes it will expand and break the pot. When overwintering containers that are not frost resistant, empty them and store them upside down. I choose to cover mine with a tarp. Pots made from cast iron and fibreglass can be left alone, as they are strong enough not to crack.

When assembling a holiday container for the winter season, use floral foam rather than soil as a base. The foam will not only retain moisture, but will also provide a firm foundation for affixing evergreen boughs and ornaments in the arrangement. Winter can be windy, so make sure you add some weight to the base: stones, sand, or broken pots will do the trick.

Getting Potty Trained

By now you know more about containers than you ever dreamed you would. But before you get planting, take a few more minutes to get to know this book. I've organized all the containers according to the season in which you'd plant them. If you pay careful attention to the headings, symbols, and instructions on each page, however, many of your containers will last longer than just one season. Here's the rundown:

Season

This tells you how long you'll want to keep the container around. Some spring containers will still look great in summer, for example, while others will be old, tired, and in need of being replaced.

Light

Those little pictures of suns tell you how much light your container will need to thrive. ☼ means full sun, which is six or more hours of direct sunlight. ☼☼ means part sun/part shade: that's about three to six hours of direct sunlight, or six hours of indirect (dappled) sunlight. Finally, ● means the container will thrive in the shade, with three or fewer hours of direct sunlight (but not darkness!).

Water

How thirsty will your container be? ♦ means you're dealing with a tough, drought-tolerant container that will need to be watered only once every few days. ♦♦ means the container will need a drink every other day or so. Finally, ♦♦♦ means you've got one thirsty container! Water it daily if you don't want to see it wither. Remember that these are just guidelines: use the finger-touch method I talked about on page 21 to see whether you may need to break the rules and water more or less often.

Description

This where I tell you how and why I picked these particular plants, and why they work so well together. This section also gives me the chance to get all poetic—try not to get too emotional when you read my flowery descriptions!

Tips and tricks

Here I give you a list of suggestions for getting the most out of this container. I'll tell you if the plants need to be pruned or deadheaded, warn you about which ones will fade first, offer ideas for freshening up the container later in the season, and let you know which plants will overwinter in your garden.

If you're a visual person like me, you'll probably pay more attention to the images splashed around each container description. We've included a close-up of each plant in the combination and told you its name and colour, so you can march right into your garden centre and ask for it. (But write your own list first—don't tear out the pages of my book!) You'll also see a symbol that looks like this: ✿. That tells you what quantity you'll need: if there are four ✿s, you need four plants for that container.

For each plant, I've told you whether it's the container's thriller, filler, or spiller. This is so you can easily make substitutions if your garden centre doesn't have the specific plant I've suggested. Just search for a similar-looking plant with the same light and water requirements, and don't be afraid to experiment.

All right now, let's pot it up!

Early Spring

Melting snow, the first robins,

the emergence of bulbs, all while the threat of Jack Frost still looms. Container gardening in early spring is all about bright colours, interesting stems, and frost-tolerant selections. Sometimes you may need to bring your pots indoors for the night—or at least cover them with a light sheet—but the cheery look of tulips, daffodils, pansies, and other early spring favourites will shake off those winter blahs.

Snappy Spring

Daffodil ('King Alfred')
Filler | ✿✿✿✿✿

SEASON: Early spring (frost tolerant)

LIGHT: ☼☼   **WATER:** 💧💧

DESCRIPTION:

Pussy willow, daffodils, and pansies are true signs of spring! The stems of pussy willow give this container a whimsical feel, while underplantings of yellow daffodils, Angelonia, and snapdragons signal the growth of spring daylight hours. 'Whiskers' pansies in yellow and blue are a story in themselves, as their happy cat-like faces welcome all those who greet this combo.

Pansy ('Whiskers')
Filler/Spiller | ✿✿✿

TIPS AND TRICKS:

- When using spring-blooming bulbs in a container, it's best to buy them already forced—this means they're already blooming in the pot. Another option is to look for prepared bulbs, which have already undergone their dormant period and can be planted in early spring.
- Willow stems are known for their ability to quickly take root: if your cuttings do end up growing roots, you can remove them and place them in your garden. Just be careful, as curly willow can easily take over.
- To extend the season of this container combo, I suggest removing the daffodils and replacing them with salvia 'Mystic Spires Blue'.
- During periods of extreme summer heat, you may find the pansies lack vigour. Trim them back to half their size with a pair of scissors and they'll bounce back vibrantly in the fall.

Snapdragon ('Yellow Luminaire')
Spiller | ✿✿

Pussy willow (cut stems)
Thriller | ✿✿✿✿✿✿

Angelonia
Filler | ✿

Early Spring

Lemon & Lime

SEASON: Early spring (frost hardy to –5°C/23°F)

LIGHT: ☼ ☼   **WATER:** 💧💧

DESCRIPTION:

One of the surest signs of the upcoming growing season is the forsythia blooming in the neighbourhood. Many gardeners use the yellow blooms as a cue to apply fertilizer to the lawn. The central colour theme of this early spring container is the warmth of yellow, complemented by the wonderful chartreuse foliage of 'Lime Rickey' coral bells. This is a bright combination that works well in large spaces: it delivers a splash of in-your-face colour.

Osteospermum ('Margarita' yellow)
Filler | ✿✿✿

TIPS AND TRICKS:

- 'Margarita' osteospermum and 'Matrix' pansies are two recent additions to that group of early-flowering plants that have a greater ability to withstand summer heat. Older varieties used to bloom in spring and fall, while remaining dormant during the heat of summer. 'Margarita', however, will bloom all season long.

- You can start parting out this container in early summer and planting osteospermum, pansies, and coral bells in the garden. You just may find that the stems of the forsythia have rooted, and you can plant these too. But remember, the mature shrub will need a space of 2 metres (6 feet) wide and 2 metres (6 feet) high. Plant it in full sun.

Heuchera (coral bells 'Lime Rickey')
Filler | ✿✿

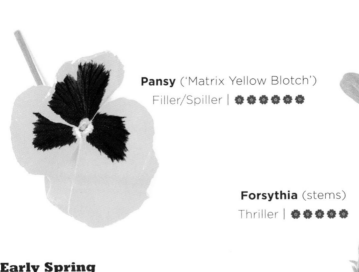

Pansy ('Matrix Yellow Blotch')
Filler/Spiller | ✿✿✿✿✿✿

Forsythia (stems)
Thriller | ✿✿✿✿✿

🌳 **Early Spring**

Cool Blue

SEASON: Early spring

LIGHT: ☼☼   **WATER:** 💧💧

DESCRIPTION:

Resourceful gardeners can create beauty from whatever they have available. Early spring is an ideal time to tour your garden—or your friends' gardens—in search of interesting stems that can be used to add some thrill to your containers. In this mix, stems of apple are planted alongside tulips, pansies, and trailing blue nemesia. Fruit trees and tulips—now that's spring! The plants in this mix are frost tolerant, but if you leave the container out during a prolonged frost you'll sacrifice the apple blossoms.

TIPS AND TRICKS:

- This container delivers a lot of impact with little effort. I created the combo simply by harvesting some apple stems from the garden, then purchasing potted tulips and a few 10 cm (4-inch) pots of nemesia and pansies.
- Although the tulips will be of no use after flowering, you may be able to transplant the nemesia and pansies in the garden. However, I would just put them in the compost pile—or, as I like to call it, the gardener's recycling bin.

Nemesia
('Innocence Opal' blue)
Spiller | ✿✿✿

Tulip (white)
Filler | ✿✿

Pansy
('Clear Blue Majestic')
Filler | ✿✿✿

Apple stem
Thriller | ✿✿✿

🌳 **Early Spring**

Sunrise

SEASON: Early spring/Spring (frost tolerant)

LIGHT: ☼ ☼   **WATER:** 💧💧

DESCRIPTION:

This mix is inspired by an early spring sunrise that warms the earth and stimulates growth everywhere. The 'Kousa' dogwood has yellowish stems that fit well with the monochromatic theme, and its interesting branching habit and newly sprouting leaves will add character to the combo. With violas, creeping Jenny, and osteospermum, this mix is not only bright but also frost tolerant.

TIPS AND TRICKS:

- This combo will last well into late spring, but once temperatures rise in summer, the viola will become leggy, the creeping Jenny will lose its vibrancy, and, like the setting sun, the whole mix will just fizzle out.
- Deadhead the osteospermum to prolong its blooms.
- The dogwood and creeping Jenny will last for years if removed and planted in the garden. Just keep in mind that creeping Jenny is a vigorous ground cover. If you ignore it, it will eventually overtake your garden.

Dogwood ('Kousa')
Thriller | ✿

Osteospermum
('Sunscape Daisy Side Show' yellow)
Filler | ✿ ✿ ✿

Lysimachia (creeping Jenny)
Spiller | ✿

Early Spring

Spring Punch

SEASON: Early spring (frost tolerant)

LIGHT: ☀ **WATER:** ♦♦♦

DESCRIPTION:

With a punch of orange and purple, this combination brightens even the dullest entranceway. The centrepiece is false spirea, whose orange-tinged and feathery leaves are complemented by the rust-coloured foliage of 'Southern Comfort' coral bells and the bicoloured blooms of the violas. The mounds of nemesia 'Angelart Orange' are the ideal filler among the coral bells and false spirea.

TIPS AND TRICKS:

- As the temperatures heat up, this combination will start to lose its appeal: the violas will stretch and the coral bells will wither. The coral bells should be removed and placed in a shady location in the garden, where they will come back year after year. Like a bottle of wine, this container won't last long, but the memories can last a lifetime.
- False spirea is an extremely vigorous growing shrub. I recommend removing it from the container in late spring and planting it in the garden.
- Nemesia will survive and thrive during the summer months. The violas, however, can be cut back by half and planted in the garden. They will return when cooler temperatures arrive in fall.

False spirea
Thriller | ✿

Viola
('Sorbet Orange Duet')
Spiller | ✿✿✿

Nemesia
('Angelart Orange')
Filler | ✿

Heuchera
(coral bells 'Southern Comfort')
Filler | ✿✿

Cherry Twig

SEASON: Early spring

LIGHT: ☼   **WATER:** 💧💧

DESCRIPTION:

Pink is a colour that makes me think of early spring. I love taking a walk through the park at this time of year to enjoy the cherry blossoms, and that's the look I've tried to capture in this container. The bright red stems of the dogwood mimic the branches of cherry trees, while the blossoms come in the form of azaleas, osteospermum, and cold-tolerant stocks in various shades of pink. Nemesia adds a nice hint of fragrance.

TIPS AND TRICKS:

- This container can take some cold, but it is not frost tolerant. On evenings that dip below the freezing mark, cover it (with burlap, a light towel, or a sheet—never plastic) or move it indoors or into a garage.
- The purple azalea dominates this mix, but its blooming period is short. I recommend enjoying this as an early-season mix and then removing the azalea and planting it in the garden. You can replace it with cherry pink geraniums or coleus—the pink or reddish foliage will give this combo long-lasting interest right through to late fall.
- 'Soprano' is only one of many varieties of osteospermum. You can substitute others, but choose one known for heat tolerance (check the plant tag). Some varieties go dormant during the summer and stop producing blooms, rebounding only in fall when temperatures drop.
- The red twig dogwood may take root in the container—you can put the rooted cutting in your garden.

Azalea ('Northern Lights')
Filler | ✿✿

Nemesia ('Innocence')
Spiller | ✿✿

Dogwood stem
Thriller | ✿✿✿

Stock (pink)
Filler | ✿✿

Osteospermum
('Soprano')
Filler | ✿✿

Early Spring

43

Crisp & Cool Kiwi

SEASON: Early spring/Spring (frost tolerant)

LIGHT: ☀ **WATER:** 💧💧💧

DESCRIPTION:

Planting a kiwi vine in a container is sure to start conversations. Who knew that kiwis could grow in Canada? This mix thrives on its simplicity: four varieties of plants with a single colour theme, anchored by the beautiful burgundy foliage of the bugleweed. Blue is a calming colour and, when used in spring, it suggests the crisp, cool mornings of the season.

TIPS AND TRICKS:

- Vines and other climbers are excellent choices for small spaces and look great when they attach themselves to a wall or weave their way through a trellis. Containers like this can be used to create privacy or to screen unsightly things, like air conditioners or your neighbour's clothesline.
- The kiwi will enjoy warmer temperatures in the summer, but the pansies and violas will not, so I recommend replacing them with black and blue annual salvia. Kiwi will overwinter in a container in Zones 4 to 9, but both kiwi and bugleweed should be placed in the ground to better the odds of overwintering success.

Ajuga
(bugleweed 'Burgundy Glow')
Spiller | ❀

Viola ('Sorbet Blue Heaven')
Filler | ❀❀

Pansy ('Clear Blue')
Filler | ❀❀❀

Kiwi vine
Thriller | ❀

Shady
Selection

Mellow Moss

SEASON: Early spring/Spring

LIGHT: ☼●   **WATER:** ♦♦♦

DESCRIPTION:

This combo celebrates spring in shady spaces. It reminds me of the forest floor in my native Ontario—although there the pansies would be replaced by white trilliums. Solomon's seal, hydrangea, and Irish moss all love the coolness of spring and don't need a lot of sun.

TIPS AND TRICKS:

- The Irish moss makes this container a fitting addition to an entranceway on St. Patty's Day, though not all garden centres will stock these plants in mid-March.
- Solomon's seal, hydrangea, and Irish moss are perennials in all but the coldest regions of Canada. Although I wouldn't recommend overwintering them in a container, you can certainly plant them in the garden in late summer.
- You'll find that this container will lack summer interest: the bloom periods of hydrangea and Solomon's seal are long gone, the heat will take its toll on the Irish moss, and the pansies will get stretched. When that happens, it's time to take this mix apart and plant the perennials in the shade garden. Then get back to the garden centre to buy new plants for a summer container.

Irish moss
Filler/Spiller | ❀ ❀

Pansy (soft yellow)
Filler | ❀ ❀ ❀

Solomon's seal
Thriller | ❀

Hydrangea ('White Ball')
Filler | ❀

Early Spring

47

Spring Rose

SEASON: Early spring (frost tolerant)

LIGHT: ☀️◐   **WATER:** 💧💧

DESCRIPTION:

Hellebore (sometimes called Christmas rose or Lenten rose) is the sizzle in this combo. In warmer climates, the foliage of this unappreciated plant remains evergreen, and it's one of the first perennials to bloom—sometimes even in late winter. In this container, its single rose-like blooms are showcased with pyramidal boxwood as the thriller, the shiny leaves of Japanese spurge as the spiller, and a covering of sphagnum moss. This combination has a natural, almost earthy feeling that reminds me of the forest floor in early spring. It's perfect for adding character to a shady corner, or it can be placed under a tree, where it will receive dappled light.

Japanese spurge ('Green Sheen')
Spiller | ❋❋

TIPS AND TRICKS:

- Hellebore is an early bloomer, but its colour is short-lived, and by late spring you will be left with a green container with very little interest. Once the threat of frost has left, you can remove the hellebores and replace them with white impatiens, creating an exceptional combo that will keep shining until fall.
- If you prefer, you can simply remove all the plants and place them in the garden once the hellebores have finished blooming. Boxwood and Japanese spurge will not easily overwinter in a container, so I recommend getting both into the ground before frost sets in during late fall. During periods of extreme summer heat, you may find the pansies lack vigour. Trim them back to half their size with a pair of scissors and they'll bounce back vibrantly in the fall.

Boxwood ('Green Gem')
Thriller | ❋

Hellebore ('Ivory Prince')
Filler | ❋❋❋

First Flowers

SEASON: Spring

LIGHT: ☼☼   **WATER:** 💧💧💧

DESCRIPTION:

Stems of magnolia, with their swelling buds, rise high above this container and promise the thrill of the season's first flowers. The theme of spring is enhanced by the huge globe-shaped blooms of hydrangea, fragrant pink hyacinth, inspiring tulips, the dainty silver foliage and pink blossoms of bog rosemary, the daisy-like flowers of osteospermum, and my favourite spring flower of all: viola in soft purple.

TIPS AND TRICKS:

- The stems of any early-flowering tree or shrub are excellent ways to add some thrill to your spring combination. You may be able to find these within your own landscapes; they're also available at most flower shops in early spring. (I don't recommend cutting them from your neighbour's tree!)
- This is a cool-season container that will survive the temperatures of late March, April, and May. But bring it indoors if you expect the mercury to dip below –5°C (23°F).
- These plants won't perform well under extreme heat, so after enjoying them in spring, compost the stems of the magnolia, tulips, and hyacinth. You can transplant the hydrangea, osteospermum, and viola after removing the spent flowers. The bog rosemary will also thrive in a garden—it's a reliable shrub that will last for many seasons.
- Water regularly and fertilize once a month with a water-soluble fertilizer formulated for flowers (such as 15-30-15).

Hydrangea (purple)
Filler | ❁

Osteospermum
('Sunscape Daisy Side Show' purple)
Filler | ❁ ❁

Viola (purple)
Filler/Spiller | ❁ ❁

Bog rosemary
Filler | ❁ ❁

Tulip (pink)
Filler | ❁

Hyacinth (pink)
Filler | ❁

Magnolia stem
Thriller | ❁ ❁

 **Early Spring**

Spring Fling

SEASON: Spring (frost tolerant)

LIGHT: ☼☀   **WATER:** 💧💧

DESCRIPTION:
This combination expresses all the subtle pleasures of spring. The curly willow stems are the fun element, while the bright yellow daffodils evoke a sense of freedom and warmth. Periwinkle, pansies, and violas add the excitement with their showy flowers. This is a happy and friendly combination that will welcome friends and family for Easter dinner.

TIPS AND TRICKS:
- This is an extremely cold-tolerant combination. All of the plants will survive freezing nights in spring and can even take a light snowfall.
- Periwinkle is a ground cover that can be removed to a perennial garden, but you can also leave it in the container and use it in a summer combination alongside shade-loving flowers. Pansies and violas are quite heat sensitive and don't perform well in summer gardens or containers.
- The stems of curly willow may take root in the container, which gives you the option of replanting them in the garden. A word of warning, however: curly willow is a monster shrub that needs at least 3 metres (10 feet) of space.
- Water regularly and fertilize once per month.

Periwinkle
Spiller | ✿✿

Daffodil ('King Alfred')
Filler | ✿✿

Viola ('Citrus Mix')
Filler | ✿✿✿

Pansy (blue and yellow)
Filler | ✿

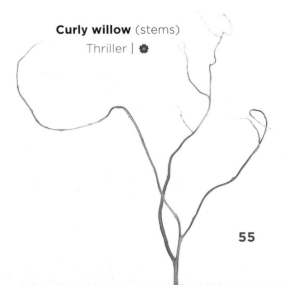

Curly willow (stems)
Thriller | ✿

Early Spring

Spring

Green grass, green leaves, popping perennials, and the hopes of a great garden season—welcome to spring! In this season, you'll enjoy the full range of choices for your containers. You still need to be concerned about the risk of frost, but you'll get to explore plants that offer plenty of blooms, interesting foliage, and even some edibles. Spring is all about promise and possibilities.

Spring Eclipse

SEASON: Spring

LIGHT: ☀ **WATER:** 💧💧💧

DESCRIPTION:

White is easy to work into any mix, and I find it spectacular when contrasting with yellow. The inspiration for this container is a solar eclipse, when the moon passes in front of the sun. The moon-like flower heads of the potted white 'Mophead' hydrangea are underplanted with the bright, sunny foliage of golden creeping Jenny, yellow pansies, and hosta. Unlike a true eclipse, there's nothing dark about this combo.

TIPS AND TRICKS:

- I would call this a cold-hardy mix, but it's not frost tolerant. Mophead hydrangeas are especially vulnerable to frost and as well as to high winds. This variety doesn't overwinter well, so enjoy it in the container and then compost it.
- Creeping Jenny and hosta are wonderful perennials for the shade garden, and both can be planted in the garden after the combo has finished its blooms.

Hosta ('August Moon')
Filler | ✿

Pansy (yellow)
Filler | ✿✿✿

Hydrangea ('Mophead')
Thriller | ✿

Lysimachia (creeping Jenny)
Spiller | ✿

Huron Sunset

SEASON: Spring/Summer

LIGHT: ☼ **WATER:** ♦♦

DESCRIPTION:

National Geographic chose the eastern shore of Lake Huron as one of the best places in the world to watch a sunset. Sitting under that sky splashed with orange, red, and yellow at the end of the day is one of my favourite memories of summer, and this simple but colourful container captures that moment. One lesson you can take away from this container is that less is often more. It includes just two plant varieties and has no thriller—the drama is in the simplicity and vibrancy of its colours.

TIPS AND TRICKS:

- Keep this combo looking great by frequently deadheading the gerbera daisies. When spent flowers are left on the plant, mildew often develops, eventually spreading to the entire container.
- In terms of performance, both Rieger begonias and gerbera daisies can be a little tricky during periods of heat and humidity. You can help with regular deadheading, but if you're a novice gardener looking for easy-to-grow varieties, I suggest a different combo.

Gerbera daisy (yellow)

Filler | ✿✿✿

Rieger begonia (bicolour)

Filler | ✿✿

Gerbera daisy (orange)

Filler | ✿✿✿

Spring

Explosion

SEASON: Spring/Summer

LIGHT: ☼   **WATER:** 💧💧

DESCRIPTION:

This busy and fun-loving container looks explosive in full sun. The mix offers a lot of punch for little effort: a diverse combination of foliage; a range of colours, from white to pink to orange; and various sizes of blooms courtesy of the dainty bougainvillea and the full-flowered petunia and geranium.

TIPS AND TRICKS:

- This is the perfect pot to tuck close to a wall. You can attach a trellis to the wall and the bougainvillea will take this mix to new heights. Placing a vine in a pot gives you the chance to soften the look of a stark wall when there is no soil near the foundation.
- Be sure to deadhead the geraniums, begonias, and nicotiana. A little "hairdressing" will keep the bougainvillea looking tidy too. Give the petunia and million bells a slight cutting in mid-summer to promote new growth right into fall.
- A word of warning: bougainvillea can attract whiteflies and aphids. Inspect the plant occasionally and spray with insecticidal soap monthly as a preventive. Any spraying, watering, and fertilizing should be done when the sun is at its lowest intensity.
- Sun-loving bougainvillea is not hardy in Canada, but it can overwinter indoors.

Bougainvillea ('Orange King')
Thriller | ❀

Geranium ('Caliente' lavender)
Filler | ❀❀❀

Wax begonia (white)
Filler | ❀❀

Nicotiana (mixed)
Filler | ❀❀❀

Calibrachoa
(million bells 'Tangerine')
Spiller | ❀❀❀

Petunia
('Easy Wave' pink)
Spiller | ❀

Spring

For the Birds

SEASON: (Spring/Summer)

LIGHT: ☼   **WATER:** 💧💧

DESCRIPTION:

This is a welcoming container that opens its arms to neighbours and friends who visit. The colour theme symbolizes friendship, warmth, and energy, and the ornamental balls and birdhouse are playful accessories. Phormium 'Waitara Gold' is similar to an ornamental grass but with wider blades—it gives wonderful character to a container, especially when it is animated by a soft breeze.

TIPS AND TRICKS:

• Accessories can turn a container from drab to fab, but they should always tie in to the central theme. In this case, I had the idea of creating a welcoming combo, but my original plant mix lacked height and I had a few open spots. The solution: I added the birdhouse for additional height, and used the balls to fill the voids.

• To maintain this container, deadhead the marigolds and nicotiana. 'Potunia' is self-cleaning, but will benefit from the occasional deadheading. Pinching (a term for pruning back annuals) the coleus will keep it in check.

Petunia ('Potunia' lime)
Spiller | 💧💧

Nicotiana (yellow)
Filler | 💧💧💧

Marigold ('Sweet Cream')
Filler | 💧💧

Coleus ('Versa Lime')
Filler | 💧💧

Phormium ('Waitara Gold')
Thriller | 💧

Lamium (spotted)
Spiller | 💧💧

Spring

Electric Shield

SEASON: Spring/Summer

LIGHT: ☼   **WATER:** ♦♦

DESCRIPTION:

The thriller in this container is the Persian shield, which inspired the overall theme. Its large leaves naturally complement the other plants with silver foliage or deep to light purple flowers. With 'Double Wave Blue Vein' petunias, purple salvia, and 'Icicles' licorice plant as monochromatic underplantings, this container needed some electricity. So I added curly willow branches twisted with florist wire to give it the appearance of lightning.

TIPS AND TRICKS:

- You can easily add interest to a container by being resourceful. The curly willow was left over from a spring mix, and the wire was lying around in my collection of garden gear (it can be purchased from any craft shop). Twenty minutes and some sore fingers later, the result was a quirky design that works for me. You could use any interesting stems or branches to create this look.
- Persian shield can get a little crazy, so an occasional pinching will maintain its overall fullness and keep your pot tidy.
- The million bells and petunias will benefit from a midsummer trim: remove at least one-third of the overall growth to stimulate fresh stems and blooms right until late fall.

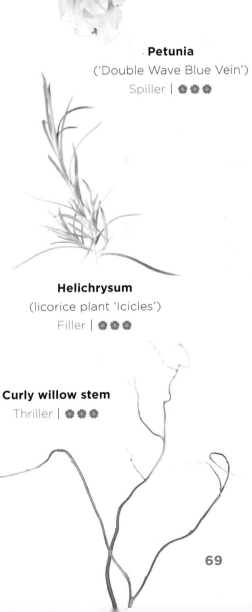

Strobilanthes
(Persian shield)
Thriller | ✿✿✿

Petunia
('Double Wave Blue Vein')
Spiller | ✿✿✿

Helichrysum
(licorice plant 'Icicles')
Filler | ✿✿✿

Calibrachoa
(million bells 'MiniFamous
Double Amethyst')
Spiller | ✿✿✿

Salvia (purple)
Filler | ✿✿✿✿

Curly willow stem
Thriller | ✿✿✿

Charisma

SEASON: Spring/Summer

LIGHT: ☼   **WATER:** 💧💧

DESCRIPTION:

Stealing its name from the variety of bower vine at its centre, this charming container is an expression of the madness of summer. With vertical growth and variegated foliage, bower vine creates a soft thrill that is complemented by the large, dark leaves of sweet potato vine spilling over the edges. Upright 'Black & Blue' salvia fill things out, while gentle white ivy geraniums and violet 'Easy Wave' petunias poke out from behind to add colour.

TIPS AND TRICKS:

- Bower vine, potato vine, 'Easy Wave' petunias, and ivy geraniums are all vigorous and easy to grow. Although this is their strength, it may also be this container's weakness, as all of them will try to dominate—especially the potato vine. I've often seen untended mixes that become just potato vine by the end of the season. To prevent this, pinch back everything to keep the mix under control.
- The petunias are self-cleaning, but the ivy geraniums are not—deadhead often for best results.

Sweet potato vine
(ipomoea 'Black Heart')
Spiller | ✿✿

Ivy geranium
('Blizzard White')
Spiller | ✿✿✿

Jasmine
(bower vine 'Charisma')
Thriller | ✿

Petunia
('Easy Wave' violet)
Spiller | ✿

Salvia
('Black & Blue')
Filler | ✿✿✿

Precious Peony

SEASON: Spring/Summer

LIGHT: ☼   **WATER:** ♦♦

DESCRIPTION:

The spectacular yellow peony flowers lead the way in this colourful planter. The rich, rosy blooms of Gaura fill out the area under the peony, while the tiny electric blue flowers of lobelia explode over the sides. I've added an accent on one side with a few blades of northern sea oats, an ornamental grass. This is one container that will let you sow your oats!

TIPS AND TRICKS:

- The 'Bartzella' peony has the beautiful double flowers and the spicy scent that are common to all varieties. The difference is that this type needs no staking: it stands tall and erect throughout the growing season, making it perfect as a cut flower. After blooming, peonies have lush foliage in a deep, dark green that will keep the back of this container interesting.
- The Gaura will fill the back of this pot with colour even after the peony is done blooming. Once a wildflower, Gaura is now cultivated as a perennial and is available in shades of pink and white. It grows up to 60 cm (2 feet) and is so light and airy that it will move with the slightest breeze. Although it looks delicate, Gaura is a tough performer that isn't bothered by pests or disease.

Lobelia (blue)
Spiller | ✽✽✽✽✽✽

Gaura (red)
Filler | ✽✽✽✽

Northern sea oats
('River Mist')
Filler | ✽

Peony ('Bartzella' yellow)
Thriller | ✽

Spring

73

Cherry Face

Hyacinth (pink)
Filler | ❀

SEASON: Spring

LIGHT: ☼☀ **WATER:** ♦♦

DESCRIPTION:

This mix of annuals, perennials, and early flowering stems uses a monochromatic colour theme with pink hyacinth, 'Purple Face' pansies, and purple sweet alyssum. Heather 'Silver Knight' ties in with this palette and offers some contrast with its foliage. Stems of cherry blossoms and spikes of perennial bergenia, with their glossy green leaves, add the height. This whimsical display is frost tolerant and even enjoys a dusting of snow.

Heather ('Silver Night')
Filler | ❀ ❀

TIPS AND TRICKS:

- On the west coast, heather retains its flowers all winter long. If you live in colder zones, you can purchase it as a potted plant and enjoy it in spring. Heather can be moved to the garden later, though I've found that its chances of survival are pretty low.
- Bergenia is easy to salvage and will do well in most part-sun gardens. Compost the cherry blossoms, pansies, and sweet alyssum; they will be well past their prime by late June.
- Water regularly and fertilize monthly.

Pansy ('Purple Face')
Filler/Spiller | ❀ ❀

Cherry stems
Thriller | ❀

Alyssum
('Clear Crystal Purple Shades')
Filler/Spiller | ❀ ❀

Bergenia (pink)
Thriller/Filler | ❀ ❀

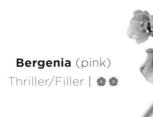

Nature's Party

SEASON: Spring

LIGHT: ☼◐ **WATER:** 💧💧

DESCRIPTION:

Robin Williams put it best when he said, "Spring is nature's way of saying, 'Let's party!'" This combination is a party in a pot. Daffodils tower above the bright blooms of purple stocks, soft yellow pansies, pink alyssum, and the soft daisy-like flowers of osteospermum. This container is a chaotic mix of opposing colours, different sizes and shapes of flowers, and an assortment of textures. It captures the energy we get from the promise of a spring day.

TIPS AND TRICKS:

- Daffodils, osteospermum, alyssum, stocks, and pansies are all cold-tolerant plants, but they don't fare well on extremely frosty nights. Cover this container with a light towel, burlap, or a sheet (never plastic) or bring it indoors or into a garage when the temperature is threatening to drop below –5°C (23°F).
- The daffodils will be the first to finish flowering. Just trim back the unsightly dead blooms and then enjoy the grass-like foliage.
- Deadhead the osteospermum, stocks, and pansies to encourage additional flowering. These plants perform well during early spring, but they will look tired when the hot weather arrives—a perfect excuse to pot up something new.
- Water regularly and fertilize monthly.

Stock (purple)
Filler | ❁

Pansy (yellow)
Filler/Spiller | ❁ ❁

Alyssum
('Clear Crystal Pink Shades')
Filler | ❁ ❁

Osteospermum (pink)
Filler | ❁ ❁ ❁

Daffodil ('King Alfred')
Thriller | ❁ ❁

 Spring

Antique Shades

SEASON: Spring

LIGHT: ☼☀   **WATER:** 💧💧

DESCRIPTION:
The velvety pink-to-silver buds of pussy willow stretch high into the sky, while the reddish blooms of 'Origami' columbine complement the burgundy and 'Antique Shades' pansies to create a combination rich in spring colour. This container will survive the cool nights of early spring and will delight you during the lengthening days of the season.

TIPS AND TRICKS:
- The thrill of this combination comes from the height of the pussy willow stems. Usually you place the tallest element of a container in the centre or at the back. Here I've shown how you can also position it to the left or right to add some asymmetry. As long as the taller plants or stems don't block the smaller ones, this may be the best way to show off their most interesting elements.
- Willow stems root easily, so you may have the opportunity to plant them after this combo is finished. However, pussy willows need a huge amount of space, so I don't recommend them for small properties.
- Columbine is an easy-to-grow perennial and should be salvaged from this combination and placed in part sun in the garden.

Pansy ('Antique Shades')
Filler | ❀❀❀

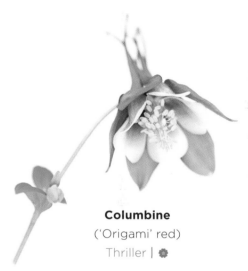

Columbine
('Origami' red)
Thriller | ❀

Pansy (burgundy)
Filler | ❀❀❀

Pussy willow
Thriller | ❀❀

 **Spring**

Hunt for Easter

SEASON: Spring/Easter

LIGHT: ☼☼   **WATER:** 💧💧

Easter lily
Thriller | ❁❁

DESCRIPTION:

The excitement of an Easter egg hunt is the theme of this combination of Easter lilies, violas, pansies, primrose, and hellebore. The plants alone capture the colour and character of the season, but the two large plastic eggs in purple and yellow really make this a fun container that kids will love.

Viola (purple)
Filler | ❁❁❁

TIPS AND TRICKS:

- The lilies and eggs in this mix shout Easter, but they also limit the appeal of this container to just that season. You may want to substitute hydrangeas and accessorize with brightly coloured ribbon in yellow, purple, pink, or green.
- Primrose and hellebore can be enjoyed in the garden for seasons to come, but the violas and pansies will fizzle out with the hot summer weather.
- Despite this being a cold-tolerant combination, it will not enjoy frost. Bring it indoors if the temperature is expected to drop below freezing.
- Water regularly and fertilize monthly.

Pansy (white)
Filler/Spiller | ❁❁❁

Primula
(primrose 'Primlet Pink Shades')
Filler | ❁❁

Pansy ('Antique Shades')
Filler/Spiller | ❁❁

Hellebore ('Ivory Prince')
Thriller/Filler | ❁

Pansy ('Purple Face')
Filler/Spiller | ❁❁❁

Spring

Delight

SEASON: Late spring/Summer

LIGHT: ☼ ☼   **WATER:** 💧💧💧

DESCRIPTION:
The fine-textured leaves of deutzia and the spiky blades of dracaena team up to add the thrill of this container. The deutzia's explosion of blossoms hovers like a cloud over the mass of colourful 'Wave' petunias and the bright pink flowers of Rieger begonia. This combination is so lush that the dainty blooms of lobelia have to fight their way through at the bottom.

TIPS AND TRICKS:
- Deutzia is a fantastic flowering shrub, but its short bloom period makes it a challenge in containers. It will finish flowering by early summer, though it will continue to offer a healthy display of foliage. In this mix, I've tried to make up for the lack of bloom by adding another foliage plant (dracaena) with a different texture and colour.
- The begonia is the only plant that will need deadheading in this combo. You should also remove the spent flowers of the deutzia, but it will not rebloom.

Lobelia ('Hot White')
Spiller | ✿ ✿

Petunia ('Wave' purple)
Spiller | ✿ ✿ ✿

Deutzia (white)
Thriller | ✿

Rieger begonia (pink)
Filler | ✿

Dracaena (green)
Thriller/Filler | ✿

Crimson Queen

SEASON: Spring/Summer/Fall

LIGHT: ☼◐ **WATER:** 💧💧

DESCRIPTION:
Few plants are as treasured as the Japanese maple—it's so exclusive that it gets a container all its own. The lacy leaves of 'Crimson Queen' in deep burgundy and dark green have an exotic effect when they rustle in the breeze. A wonderful addition to an urban patio, this plant will give your home a sophisticated look.

TIPS AND TRICKS:
- Like many Japanese maples, this variety evolves over the seasons: the sweeping foliage is a spectacular green and burgundy in spring and summer, and then the cooler temperatures and shorter days of fall turn the leaves a brilliant red.
- Something this beautiful does not come cheap. This planter is a major investment (about $200), so it will need extra care to overwinter. It's best to plant it in the ground or bring it into a garage or cold cellar where it can undergo a period of dormancy with cool temperatures and minimal light.

Simple Solution

Japanese maple
('Crimson Queen')
Thriller | ❀

Purity Purple

SEASON: Spring

LIGHT: ☀ **WATER:** 💧💧💧

DESCRIPTION:

Sometimes the best container combos create themselves, so keep your eyes open at the garden centre. If you go with a fixed idea, you may be inclined to buy unhealthy or unattractive plants simply because they fit your colour scheme. With this container, the Japanese painted fern was my inspiration: it was the first plant I gravitated toward, and within its foliage I could see white and purple. Presto—this feminine mix was created. The large white "powder puffs" of the hydrangea are complemented by the white osteospermum. Both contrast with the vibrant purple of the pansies and stocks, and everything is tied together by the fern.

TIPS AND TRICKS:

- This is a cold-tolerant mix, but it definitely won't take frost. If there's a threat of frost overnight, cover the container with a light sheet, burlap, or a towel (never plastic), or bring it indoors or into a garage.
- When the hydrangea flowers are spent, replace with white 'Rocky Mountain' geraniums. Mophead hydrangea is mainly an indoor plant—you could move it to the garden, but it rarely does well.
- In time you'll find the pansies will get leggy. Just grab a pair of scissors and cut them back by half. They will rebound when temperatures cool.
- In fall remove the painted ferns and plant in the garden to ensure overwintering success. If you want to use them again next season, leave them in the container and plant the whole pot in the garden so they can be easily removed next spring.

Stock ('Hot Cakes' purple)
Filler | ✿✿✿

Hydrangea ('Mophead')
Thriller | ✿

Pansy (purple)
Filler | ✿✿✿

Osteospermum
('Sunscape Daisy Side Show' white)
Filler | ✿✿✿✿

Japanese painted fern ('Pictum')
Filler/Spiller | ✿✿

Spring

Velvet Beauty

SEASON: Spring

LIGHT: ☀   **WATER:** 💧💧💧

DESCRIPTION:

I like to use foliage to showcase other flowering plants, and to tie combinations together. I love coral bells, and the dark, velvety foliage of 'Black Beauty' helps show off the blooms of hydrangea, nemesia, and dianthus. Its flower heads also look great when they gently spring up through the dominant 'Bright Light' hydrangea.

TIPS AND TRICKS:

- This container will hold up well during cool summers, but eventually the hydrangea's blooms will fade and lose their appeal. I recommend replacing it with pink geraniums, cherry oleander, coleus, or pink bougainvillea.
- 'Bright Light' hydrangea is intended for indoors, though you can try overwintering it in the garden if you live within Zones 5 to 9.
- In fall remove the 'Black Beauty' coral bells, as it is a perennial and can be enjoyed for years to come if overwintered in the garden.

Dianthus
('Super Trooper Velvet & White')
Filler | ❀❀❀

Heuchera
(coral bells 'Black Beauty')
Filler | ❀

Hydrangea ('Bright Light')
Thriller | ❀

Nemesia ('Aromatica Rose Pink')
Spiller | ❀❀

Candy Cone Cascade

SEASON: Spring

LIGHT: ☀ **WATER:** 💧💧💧

DESCRIPTION:

This container was inspired by my son eating an ice cream cone. The pink hydrangea resembles a scoop of strawberry ice cream, while the cascading alyssum reminds me of melting vanilla. Like the arrival of an ice cream truck on a hot summer day, this big, bright combo will make the whole neighbourhood happy.

Marguerite daisy
('Courtyard Buttercream')
Filler | ❀❀❀

TIPS AND TRICKS:

- I was amazed how long this combo lasted in front of my mother's home. Plunked outside the garage, directly on pavement with northern exposure, this container performed well for weeks.
- Although it's not frost tolerant, this container will take cold temperatures. However, because the hydrangea heads are so large, I recommend keeping it out of windy locations. You may also want to place some stones in the base of the pot for stability.
- This really is an annual container: the hydrangea may overwinter in the garden, but my feeling is that once it has finished blooming, you can place it in the compost pile.

Stock ('Hot Cakes' white)
Filler | ❀❀❀

Alyssum ('Snow Princess')
Spiller | 💧💧💧

Hydrangea ('Bright Light')
Thriller | ❀❀❀

Spring Sense

SEASON: Spring

LIGHT: ☀ **WATER:** 💧💧

DESCRIPTION:

Kids love this simple mix. The plants in this combo celebrate the senses of smell and touch and can bring kids one step closer to nature—and one step farther from the computer! Fragrant viburnum produces a wonderful perfume to celebrate spring, while the silver foliage of dusty miller has a velvety texture, despite its frosty appearance.

TIPS AND TRICKS:

- This may not be the showiest of mixes—especially after the viburnum completes its bloom period—but it will thrive in a part-sun location all season long.
- In fall viburnum will be the perfect addition to the flower garden—or use it in a new fall combo, as its foliage will take on a reddish hue and give one last show before it snows.
- Viburnum and periwinkle are tough perennials and it wouldn't surprise me if they overwintered in a container, even in Zone 3. However, to be safe, n them to the garden in late summer.

Dusty miller
Filler | ✿✿✿

Fragrant viburnum
Thriller | ✿

Periwinkle
Spiller | ✿✿

Pansy (white)
Filler | ✿✿✿

Nemesia
('Aromatica White')
Filler/Spiller | ✿✿

 **Spring**

Earth Cracker

SEASON: Late spring/Summer

LIGHT: ☼ **WATER:** 💧💧

DESCRIPTION:
'Potunia Cappuccino' is a new variety of petunia that's ideal for containers. The flowers' deep centres and creamy brown edges are a perfect fit with 'Mahogany' coral bells and the foliage of the dark leaf canna. By late summer the red blooms of the canna will tower above the planter like a torch held high. The fuchsia—I've selected a variety called honeysuckle or 'Firecracker' fuchsia—adds colour to this earthy combo all season long.

TIPS AND TRICKS:
- Cannas are an absolute thriller—their tall stature and huge leaves make a dramatic impression. However, they're also effective wind catchers, so before you plant this combo, place some rocks in the bottom of the container to weigh it down. There is nothing more frustrating than seeing your planter toppled day after day.
- Late in the season, 'Potunia Cappuccino' tends to look a little tired. To jolt these guys back to life, give them a haircut, cutting back about half of their growth. Within 10 days, your Edward Scissorhands technique will reward you with new growth and increased bloom production right through till frost.
- 'Mahogany' coral bells are one of the few heat-tolerant varieties that are perennial to Zone 4, so in fall you can move them into the garden for overwintering.
- The canna tubers can be removed and stored indoors in a cool, dark, dry place. If you start them indoors in late March, you can reuse them in your containers in spring.

Canna (red)
Thriller | ❁

Fucshia ('Firecracker')
Filler | ❁❁❁

Heuchera
(coral bells 'Mahogany')
Filler | ❁❁

Petunia
('Potunia Cappuccino')
Spiller | ❁❁❁

 Spring

Spike Berry

SEASON: Late spring/Summer

LIGHT: ☼   **WATER:** 💧💧

Cordyline (red)
Thriller | ✿

DESCRIPTION:

The thriller in this combo—the familiar spikes of cordyline (also known as Hawaiian Ti plant)—may not be all that thrilling on its own. But the red foliage of this variety works well with the pink geraniums and the cherry pink gerbera daisies. The underplanting of dracaena, whose foliage has both red and pink tones, helps tie the mix together. The pink-flowering strawberries will eventually spill over the pot—this container is not just ornamental, it's edible too.

TIPS AND TRICKS:

- 'Pretty in Pink' is an ever-bearing variety of strawberry that flowers from early spring until frost and continuously produces small, soft, and somewhat tart fruit. Planted in the garden, it makes a great perennial ground cover.

Gerbera daisy (pink)
Filler | ✿✿

- Both cordyline and dracaena are "patio tropicals," which means that you should bring them indoors for overwintering. My uncle has been overwintering his spikes for 10 years and they are over 2 metres (6 feet) high.

- To reduce the risk of powdery mildew and increase bloom production, remove spent flowers on the gerbera daisies immediately.

Ivy geranium
('Colorcade' pink)
Spiller | ✿✿✿

Strawberry ('Pretty in Pink')
Spiller | ✿✿

Dracaena ('Marginata' red)
Filler | ✿✿

Coral Collection

SEASON: Spring/Summer/Fall

LIGHT: ☀ **WATER:** ♦♦

DESCRIPTION:
One type of plant in four different varieties creates a simple but stunning container. Coral bells come in several forms, from the dark foliage of 'Obsidian' to the unique deep green veining of 'Green Spice' to the vibrant reddish leaves of 'Mahogany' and 'Midnight Rose'. The only thing that coral bells lack is showy flowers (their blooms are tiny), so I've added an ornamental flower as an accessory to play that role.

TIPS AND TRICKS:
- Coral bells, hosta, and even bleeding heart are examples of perennials that come in an array of varieties, and these can be combined in interesting containers. Sticking to one plant type can be successful, but it does come with a risk: a bout of weather, insects, or disease can attack everything at once. In this case, you don't need to worry—coral bells are almost bulletproof.
- Coral bells are perennials, but they don't overwinter well in pots. Plant them in the garden in late fall.
- Regular watering and monthly fertilizing are all the care this container will need.

Heuchera (coral bells 'Obsidian')
Filler | ✿

Heuchera (coral bells 'Mahogany')
Filler | ✿

Heuchera (coral bells 'Green Spice')
Filler | ✿✿

Heuchera (coral bells 'Midnight Rose')
Filler | ✿

 **Spring**

Summer

Sweltering temperatures, long

periods without rain, the fiery colours of heat-loving plants, and the taste of fresh vine-ripened tomatoes—these are the hot, hazy, lazy days of summer. Now your challenge in the container garden is survival: you'll be using plants with long-lasting blooms, drought tolerance, and cool-looking tropical foliage you can enjoy from the edge of the pool.

Pretoria Lime

SEASON: Summer

LIGHT: ☼   **WATER:** 💧💧

DESCRIPTION:

Chartreuse has always been a fave of mine. Back in my single days I even painted my kitchen this colour. (It was the first thing my wife repainted.) The reason for my affection for this colour is how well it works with many variations of green and yellow. Here the big-brimmed cannas and the fringed foliage of coleus partner with the bright blooms of Rieger begonias and the heart-shaped leaves of 'Sidekick Lime' sweet potato vine to give this container texture as well as incredible colour, both of which add excitement and warmth, especially when placed beside an entrance or pool.

TIPS AND TRICKS:

• This heat-loving combo will be challenged by the vigorous growth of the potato vine, which is notorious for overtaking entire containers by summer's end. Pinch yours back regularly to keep it in check.

• In late summer the coleus will also benefit from an occasional pinching to create good shape and encourage new growth.

• 'Pretoria' cannas can be overwintered: remove their tubers in early fall and store them indoors in a cool, dark, dry location.

Sweet potato vine
(ipomoea 'Sidekick Lime')
Spiller | ✿✿✿

Rieger begonia (yellow)
Filler | ✿✿

Coleus ('Sunlover')
Filler | ✿✿

Canna ('Pretoria')
Thriller | ✿

Orange Marmalade

SEASON: Summer

LIGHT: ☼   **WATER:** ♦♦

DESCRIPTION:

All the sizzle of summer comes together in this monochromatic combo. 'Tango Orange' geraniums are underplanted with peach-flowering verbena and complemented by 'Marmalade' coral bells. Some say that orange represents endurance and vitality, and that holds true here. This whole selection can thrive in the heat of summer. 'Tiara' is one of the few verbena varieties that are mildew resistant.

TIPS AND TRICKS:

- Deadhead, deadhead, deadhead! This container will perform well all summer as long as you remove spent flowers on the geraniums and verbena. Flowering annuals devote most of their energy toward bloom production, so by deadheading and fertilizing you'll redirect that energy to the foliage and roots. And as I like to say, with happy bottoms you always have happy tops.
- Remove the coral bells and plant them in the garden in early fall. Both the verbena and geraniums can be tossed in the compost pile.

Heuchera (coral bells 'Marmalade')
Filler | ✿

Verbena ('Tiara' orange ánd red)
Spiller | ✿✿✿

Geranium ('Tango Orange')
Thriller | ✿

Imperial Punch

SEASON: Summer

LIGHT: ☼   **WATER:** 💧💧

DESCRIPTION:

This is a container fit for a king. It creates a royal feel with rich combinations of deep purple, cherry, and blue, topped by the stately 'Imperial Taro', with its elephant ear–like leaves. The punchy flowers of the geraniums, the rich double blooms of the 'Wave' petunias and the compact, multiflowering stems of million bells contrast with the dark foliage, adding to the regal texture.

TIPS AND TRICKS:

- 'Wave' petunias and million bells are known as self-cleaners, but I'd still encourage you to continually deadhead all the flowering plants in this mixture. I also suggest cutting back the petunias and million bells by half in late summer; this will promote a flush of new growth and greater performance through to fall.
- You can remove the colocasia tubers in late fall (after frost) and store them indoors in a cool, dark, dry location.

Colocasia ('Imperial Taro')
Thriller | ❁

Petunia ('Double Wave' purple)
Spiller | ❁❁

Calibrachoa (million bells blue)
Spiller | ❁❁

Geranium ('Rocky Mountain')
Filler | ❁❁

Tangerine

SEASON: Summer

LIGHT: ☼   **WATER:** ♦♦

DESCRIPTION:
Hibiscus has always been associated with tropical climates, where palms swa
in the warm winds. In this container, the dwarf giant papyrus replaces th
palms, and the deep peach blooms of million bells 'Tangerine' make a perfe
partner. For me, this mix brings back poolside memories—the only thing miss
ing is my all-inclusive bar tab.

TIPS AND TRICKS:
- Hibiscus is known for attracting aphids and whiteflies. To prevent these pest
  give the plant an occasional spray of insecticidal soap during the summer.
- In the fall, remove the million bells and papyrus, but leave the hibiscus i
  the pot. Give it one final spray with insecticidal soap, then bring it indoors
  and place it in a room with bright light (west or south). Water it only when it's
  dry, and cut back on fertilizer from October to March, during the time when
  daylight hours are at a minimum.

Calibrachoa
(million bells 'Tangerine')
Spiller | ✿✿✿

Hibiscus (peach)
Thriller/Filler | ✿

Cyperus
(dwarf giant papyrus 'King Tut')
Thriller | ✿✿

Hurricane

SEASON: Summer

LIGHT: ☼   **WATER:** 💧💧

DESCRIPTION:
Hurricanes pack a powerful punch, and so do this container's bright colours. This mix features orange gerbera daisies and red hibiscus rising above the bold blooms of 'Caloha Cherry' million bells. Just as a storm eventually gives way to a gentle calm, this container gets a relaxed feel from the stately, swaying stems of 'King Tut'.

TIPS AND TRICKS:
- Gerbera daisies require immediate deadheading, as rotting blooms can easily send disease spreading through this container.
- Continually monitor the hibiscus for whiteflies and aphids. The occasional spraying of insecticidal soap will help prevent them. You can bring this plant indoors over the winter, but remember to treat it with insecticidal soap first.
- Million bells will greatly benefit from a late-season pinching to get rid of the tired growth and help stimulate new blooms until the killing frost.

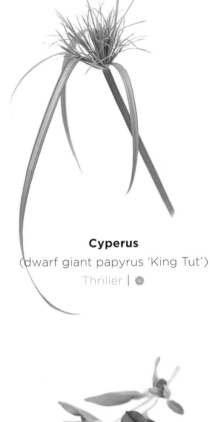

Cyperus
(dwarf giant papyrus 'King Tut')
Thriller | ✿

Calibrachoa
(million bells 'Caloha Cherry')
Spiller | ✿✿✿

Gerbera daisy (orange)
Filler | ✿✿✿

Hibiscus (red)
Thriller/Filler | ✿

Big Tropical Impact

Caliente Pazazz

SEASON: Summer

LIGHT: ☼   **WATER:** 🌢🌢

DESCRIPTION:

Hot and sexy are the best words to describe this combo. The ornamental banana is the centrepiece, and it immediately suggests a tropical destination, while the succulent leaves of purslane boil over from the edges. This container not only looks hot but likes it hot: ivy geraniums, purslane, and banana do best during sweltering summers—the more the mercury spikes, the better they will grow. And unlike many varieties of coleus, the 'Stained Glassworks' family loves the sun too.

TIPS AND TRICKS:

- Big and bold banana is not a fan of winds. The plant's large leaves whip in the breeze and will get torn to shreds—or they will act as sails, and if not properly weighted, the container will easily topple over.
- Treat banana as a tropical plant and it can be enjoyed for many seasons to come. Bring it indoors in early fall, before the warning of frost. (Spray it first with a weak solution of insecticidal soap.) Place the plant in a bright room, but not directly in front of a window. Allow the plant to dry between waterings. Bananas love having some moisture in the air, so use a humidifier in the room.
- Deadhead the dahlietta and ivy geranium, and give the coleus an occasional pinching to keep it under control.

Portulaca
(purslane 'Pazazz Salmon Glow')
Spiller | 🌢🌢

Coleus
('Stained Glassworks Tilt-a-Whirl')
Filler | 🌢🌢

Banana tree
Thriller | 🌢

Dahlietta (yellow and orange)
Filler | 🌢🌢

Geranium ('Caliente' orange)
Filler | 🌢

Rosy Heights

SEASON: Summer

LIGHT: ☼   **WATER:** 💧💧

DESCRIPTION:
The combo delivers a knockout punch. 'Knock Out' is a trade name for a variety of standard rose known for disease and insect resistance, and for its continuous bloom. (Actually, in this picture the rose is not in bloom, but the tips of new growth tie nicely into the underplantings.) In its glory, this container is a passionate explosion of pink from top to bottom, including the variegated foliage of Gaura.

TIPS AND TRICKS:
- There is a reason standard roses are grown in a pot: it's easier to overwinter them. Standards (also known as tree roses) are difficult to overwinter outdoors, as their graft point is high above soil level and easily exposed to killing cold temperatures. The portability of a container allows you to easily bring yours into an insulated garage or cold cellar.
- If you do overwinter the rose, prune it back by a third and remove any dead or weak canes in late fall. When you bring it out again in spring, give it another pruning.
- 'Knock Out' roses are disease and insect resistant, but they aren't necessarily free of these pests. Inspect them for aphids and for overall health, and give them an occasional spray of insecticidal soap.
- This container may require relatively frequent watering and fertilizing for peak performance. It is also helpful to weigh the pot down in breezy locations to keep it from toppling.

Gaura ('Passionate Rainbow')
Filler | ✿ ✿ ✿

Petunia (pink)
Filler | ✿ ✿

Verbena ('Lascar Dark Pink')
Spiller | ✿ ✿ ✿

Standard rose ('Knock Out')
Thriller | ✿

Summer Spice

SEASON: Summer

LIGHT: ☼   **WATER:** 💧💧

DESCRIPTION:
Using cayenne peppers as the centrepiece makes this one hot combo. New Guinea impatiens (often called sunshine impatiens), marigolds, and orange zinnias also sizzle in this summer mix, while the spill of 'Sweet Caroline Bronze' potato vine signals that fall is right around the corner. This combo would suit a lover of spicy food or Mexican culture, but be careful to keep the hot peppers out of the reach of young children.

TIPS AND TRICKS:
- The stems of the cayenne pepper will require some staking to keep them upright. Pepper plants are also notorious for attracting whiteflies, but the companion planting of marigolds here should help repel both them and aphids. To be safe, though, give the plant an occasional spray of insecticidal soap.
- Marigolds and zinnias require deadheading, but the impatiens are self-cleaning. The potato vine grows vigorously, so pinch it back to keep it under control.
- This container will need frequent watering.

Cayenne pepper (red)
Thriller | ✿

Marigold ('Bonanza Flame')
Filler | ✿✿✿✿✿✿

Zinnia (orange)
Filler | ✿✿

Sweet potato vine
(ipomoea 'Sweet Caroline Bronze')
Spiller | ✿✿

New Guinea impatiens (orange)
Filler | ✿✿

Rubin's Egg

SEASON: Summer

LIGHT: ☼   **WATER:** ♦♦

DESCRIPTION:

This tasty combo is an instant conversation starter. Edibles such as 'Little Fingers' eggplant are often overlooked for mixed containers. But with interesting foliage, purple flowers, and unique fruit, eggplant offers more than your typical thriller. The colourful and flavourful 'Red Rubin' basil flanks the edible flowers of nasturtiums and the big, bold blooms of marigolds. Together, they're a tasty treat for the eyes and stomach.

TIPS AND TRICKS:

- 'Little Fingers' eggplant is perfect for containers. However, it will require some staking to support the weight of its fruit.
- This container is a lesson in companion planting. Nasturtiums attract insects that consume their leaves and flowers, but these bugs then leave the other plants alone. (Nasturtiums grow quickly, so insect damage is not that noticeable.) Also, the eggplant, marigolds, and nasturtiums shelter the basil from wind.
- The marigolds and nasturtiums will benefit from regular deadheading. The best way to improve the health of the basil is to cut some regularly, even if you don't need it for your food. If you allow the basil to go to seed or overgrow, it will weaken the overall health of the plant. But don't overdo it: trim only a third of the plant at a time.

Marigold ('Antigua' yellow)
Filler | ❀ ❀ ❀ ❀

Basil ('Red Rubin')
Filler | ❀ ❀

Eggplant ('Little Fingers')
Thriller | ❀

Nasturtium (mixed)
Spiller | ❀ ❀

Summer

Sweet and Simple

SEASON: Summer

LIGHT: ☼   **WATER:** ◗◗

DESCRIPTION:

Perilla 'Tricolor' isn't the thriller in this container, but it's the anchor and the inspiration—I selected the companion plants based on its colours. The foliage is a combination of pinks, purples, red, and lime green. This easily ties in with the sections of lime-green potato vine, violet 'Wave' petunias, and pink Mandevilla. The lush look of this combination creates a tropical feel, complemented by the thick bamboo pole that provides support for the Mandevilla. The result is outstanding colour—both in foliage and in flower.

Petunia ('Easy Wave' violet)
Filler/Spiller | ✿ ✿

TIPS AND TRICKS:

- The challenge of this container is keeping it under control. Mandevilla is a fast-growing vine, potato vine is a vigorous spiller, and Perilla and 'Wave' petunias are monster fillers. Occasionally pinching the potato vine, Perilla, and petunias will keep your container looking its best. If you neglect this task, by the end of the season you'll likely have a pot of potato vine, with the Mandevilla struggling for space.
- Using vines in containers offers an opportunity to create portable vertical spaces. By placing your container close to a fence, or any structure that would allow a vine to wind through, your container will become the launch pad for a beautiful display all season long.
- Mandevilla is a patio tropical that can be overwintered, but be careful not to bring aphids or whiteflies indoors. Spray with insecticidal soap first.

Perilla ('Tricolor')
Filler | ✿ ✿

Sweet potato vine (ipomoea 'Sweet Georgia' light green)
Filler/Spiller | ✿ ✿

Mandevilla
('Sun Parasol Pretty Pink')
Thriller | ✿

Summer

Lemon Jenny

SEASON: Summer

LIGHT: ☼   **WATER:** 💧💧

DESCRIPTION:

Lemon Jenny is a combination that spreads up, out, and over. The thrill of this container comes from the bower vine's variegated foliage and its pink trumpet-shaped flowers that bloom during the hottest of weather. These combine well with the plum-coloured 'Wave' petunias that spill over the edge. Complementing the entire container are soft, yellow-flowering 'Sweet Cream' marigolds, blue ageratum, cream lantana, and 'Golden Globes'.

TIPS AND TRICKS:

- Normal is boring! I like to give traditional things an innovative spin, and that's the goal of the obelisk I selected for this container. It reminds me of a jet rocketing into the sky and adds vertical drama to the mix.
- Sometimes plant support systems are ornamental as well as functional. The obelisk gives this container a strong . . . er . . . masculine look. This is a container I would have placed in front of my home during my bachelor days.
- Deadheading, training, and pinching the bower vine—as well as regular fertilizing—will keep this mix exploding all summer long. The bower vine can even be overwintered: bring it indoors before hard frost.

Marigold ('Sweet Cream')
Filler | ✿✿✿

Petunia
('Easy Wave' blue)
Spiller | ✿✿

Lantana
('Lucky Lemon Cream')
Filler | ✿✿✿

Jasmine
(bower vine variegated)
Thriller | ✿

Ageratum (blue)
Filler | ✿✿✿

Lysimachia
('Golden Globes')
Spiller | ✿✿✿

Tangerine Crackle

SEASON: Summer

LIGHT: ☼   **WATER:** ♦♦

DESCRIPTION:

This container crackles with big, bold, bright foliage, brilliant flowers, and the spill of millions of tangerine trumpets. 'Pretoria' canna makes a huge impression; this summer-flowering tuber will grow quickly with enough heat (it will struggle in cooler conditions). If you look closely at the photo, you'll notice a vine climbing the canna for support: black-eyed Susan is a sun-loving annual vine that will grow well with minimal space.

TIPS AND TRICKS:

- As long as Mother Nature provides the warmth, this container will grow big—and fast. The bigger the plants, the more food they will need, so I recommend regular watering and fertilizing at half-strength every week.
- The canna will grow quickly enough to provide the support for the black-eyed Susan vine, though initially you will want to help it find the right direction—if not, Susie will grow anywhere and everywhere.
- Deadheading the fuchsia and occasionally cutting back the million bells will help promote healthier plants.
- You can overwinter the canna by uprooting the tubers, allowing the soil to dry and gently brushing them clean. Cut off the foliage, place the tubers in vermiculite or peat moss, and store them in a cool, dark, dry place over the winter.

Canna
('Pretoria' variegated)
Thriller | ✿

Fuchsia ('Firecracker')
Filler | ✿✿

Coleus
('Stained Glassworks')
Filler | ✿

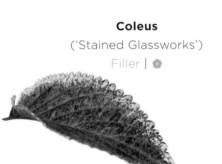

Calibrachoa
(million bells 'Tangerine')
Spiller | ✿✿

Black-eyed Susan vine (orange)
Thriller/Filler | ✿✿

Summer

Loves It Hot!

Kool Kangaroo

SEASON: Summer

LIGHT: ☼   **WATER:** ◐

DESCRIPTION:

This simple combination—with the help of a simple, inexpensive accessory—mixes orange and green with hints of brown and copper. The intended thriller—the 'Red Dragon' hibiscus—will be front and centre when it's in bloom. However, the coleus and kangaroo paw fill the void. The purslane spills over and offers continual blooms of salmon-to-orange single flowers. I twisted copper florist wire into spring-like shapes to offer a surprise of additional colour and texture, and to inspire conversation.

TIPS AND TRICKS:

- This is a real sun-loving combination. The hibiscus and kangaroo paw love to bask in the heat, and drought-tolerant purslane thrives in the sunniest spots. You don't need to worry about the coleus, either—'Versa' is one of the varieties that thrive in full sun.
- Monitor the hibiscus for diseases such as black spot, or insects like aphids and whiteflies. If you notice a problem, treat it with a fungicide-insecticide combination.
- Almost all the plants in this combo will survive with minimal fertilizer. But for best results, fertilize monthly or add a slow-release, granular all-season fertilizer at planting.
- Both the hibiscus and the kangaroo paw can be brought indoors before the risk of hard frost.

Coleus
('Versa Burgundy to Green')
Filler | ✿

Hibiscus ('Red Dragon')
Thriller | ✿

Anigozanthos
(kangaroo paw 'Kanga Orange')
Thriller | ✿

Portulaca
(purslane 'Pazazz Salmon Glow')
Spiller | ✿ ✿ ✿

Rusty

SEASON: Summer

LIGHT: ☼   **WATER:** 💧💧

DESCRIPTION:

This container is all about fantastic foliage. The coppery leaves and deep burgundy veining of the sweet potato vine tie in naturally with the dramatic canna. Just these two plants would make an awesome combo, but things get even better with the waxy leaves of 'Dragon Wing' begonia alongside the dark foliage of 'Nonstop Mocca'. The orange blooms of the tuberous begonia will pop to the forefront, while the dainty flowers of 'Dragon Wing' fill the background.

TIPS AND TRICKS:

• A well-designed container is interesting even without flowers—that's the lesson here. When selecting plants, imagine them when they're not in bloom, and if they lack interest, you may want to reconsider. During the growing season there will be periods when some plants do not flower, perhaps because of temperature or weather patterns. If your selection looks great based on foliage alone, the blooms are just a bonus.

• 'Dragon Wing' begonias are near the top of my list of foolproof plants. This annual may look unattractive when it's small, but by the end of the season it is always one of the last surviving plants, even with minimal care.

• If you're looking to save a few bucks next season, you can lift the canna tubers in fall, store them indoors, and replant them in the spring.

Tuberous begonia
('Nonstop Mocca Deep Orange')
Filler | ✿✿✿

Canna ('Australia')
Thriller | ✿✿

Sweet potato vine (ipomoea
'Sweet Caroline Bronze')
Spiller | ✿✿

Begonia ('Dragon Wing' red)
Filler | ✿

Summer

100% Edible

Saucy!

SEASON: Summer

LIGHT: ☼   **WATER:** ♦♦

DESCRIPTION:

This edible delight is a combination of my three favourite foods: basil, tomatoes, and oregano. If this sounds like the start of the ultimate pasta sauce or summer salad, you're right. This container is functional, but it's also colourful. 'Red Rubin' basil contrasts nicely with the light green foliage of sweet basil, and the smaller leaf size of 'Spicy Globe' offers some interest with its unique form. Fresh tomatoes ripening on the vine will draw your eye to the top, while the Greek oregano spills over the sides to fill the bottom.

TIPS AND TRICKS:

- Tomatoes are the perfect edible plant to grow in containers if you lack space, or if you just want to experiment with vegetable gardening before ripping up the front yard. When selecting tomatoes for containers, choose indeterminate varieties (also called bush-type or patio varieties), as they stay compact. If you can't find 'Better Bush', look for 'Better Boy' or 'Early Girl'.
- Avoid placing this pot in a windy area, especially early in the season, as there is nothing sweet basil and 'Red Rubin' hate more than cold wind.
- As the stem of the tomato plant thickens, suckers (side shoots) will appear in the crotch between the stem and the branches. Pinch these off (just use your fingertips) to direct the plant's energy into producing more tomatoes instead of more foliage.
- Harvest both basil and oregano frequently, as this will help promote new vigorous growth.
- Some gardeners swear that an underplanting of basil improves the flavour of tomatoes. Personally, I can't tell the difference but, heck, it's worth a try.

Greek oregano
Filler | ✿✿✿

Basil ('Red Rubin')
Filler | ✿✿

Basil
('Spicy Globe')
Filler | ✿

Sweet basil
Filler | ✿

Tomato ('Better Bush')
Thriller | ✿

Summer

141

Stained Glass

SEASON: Summer

LIGHT: ☼   **WATER:** ◆

DESCRIPTION:
This container is full of fun, even without a flower in sight. Hibiscus 'Powder Puff' does offer fantastic yellow double flowers with light pink centres, but even when it's not in bloom its leaves contrast spectacularly with the dark foliage of coleus 'Molten Lava' and the orange-to-rust leaves of coleus 'Tilt-a-Whirl'. These three sun-loving plants make ideal partners, offering enough diversity to create a simple yet pleasing combination.

TIPS AND TRICKS:
- Coleus should be even more popular than it is. Easy to grow, with both sun- and shade-loving varieties, these plants offer so many colour choices and leaf shapes that they create almost an infinite number of combinations. Occasionally, coleus is so "easy" that you'll have to hold it back. Pinch it regularly to keep it from dominating the container.
- Hibiscus 'Powder Puff' can be moody, and when we shot this photo it was too stubborn to flower. The lesson here is that as long as you use contrasting foliage, a container will still look great without blooms.
- Bring the hibiscus indoors before the risk of frost in fall, but spray it with insecticidal soap first.

Coleus
('Stained Glassworks Tilt-a-Whirl')
Filler | ❀❀❀

Hibiscus ('Powder Puff')
Thriller | ❀

Coleus
('Stained Glassworks Molten Lava')
Filler | ❀❀❀

Indian Summer

SEASON: Summer/Fall

LIGHT: ☼   **WATER:** 💧💧

DESCRIPTION:

The burgundy foliage and corn-like stature of 'Jester' millet give this combination the look and feel of a late-summer harvest. That theme continues with the late-arriving flowers of 'Cherry Brandy' rudbeckia, 'Magellan Scarlet' zinnia, and the dried texture of the blooms of strawflower. This combination of red, yellow, and orange creates a real warmth that will make you think of the mild fall days ahead as the summer evenings start to cool.

TIPS AND TRICKS:

- A challenge with any container is timing: you want your pot to be blooming with colour when you need it. Try to group plants with similar bloom times (check the plant tags when you're at the garden centre). This pot is geared directly to late summer and fall, so earlier in the season it may lack colour because the rudbeckia is not in bloom and the millet has not formed its plumes (seed heads). You may want to keep it in a less prominent area in early summer before moving it to centre stage later in the season.
- To develop its deep burgundy colour, 'Jester' millet must be in full sun. If you place this container in low light, you may notice the foliage is more chartreuse to green.
- Deadhead the strawflower, zinnia, and rudbeckia, and remove the drying foliage of the millet.

Millet ('Jester')
Thriller | ✿

Zinnia ('Magellan Scarlet')
Filler | ✿✿

Bracteantha
(strawflower yellow)
Spiller | ✿✿✿

Rudbeckia ('Cherry Brandy')
Filler | ✿✿

Summer

Water
Wise

Desert Blue

SEASON: Summer

LIGHT: ☼   **WATER:** ⬤

DESCRIPTION:

A clear blue sky can mean rainless days and periods of drought. With that theme in mind, this combo is a selection of blue to silver foliage plants that are extremely drought tolerant. Ornamental grasses and a collection of succulents combine with licorice plant to create the ideal container for water-wise (or lazy!) gardeners. It's an ideal choice for anyone who has a sunny spot and spends a lot of time away.

TIPS AND TRICKS:

- Other than the occasional watering, this container is easy—it doesn't even need fertilizing. The only thing it needs is full sun.
- The three perennials (switch grass, fescue, and stonecrop) can be planted in the garden and enjoyed for years to come, but the licorice plant will end up in the compost pile.

Fescue ('Elijah Blue')
Filler/Spiller | ✿ ✿ ✿

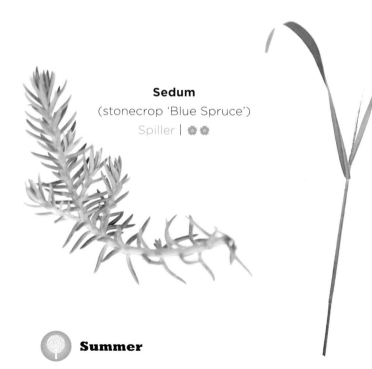

Sedum
(stonecrop 'Blue Spruce')
Spiller | ✿ ✿

Switch grass
('Prairie Sky')
Thriller | ✿

Helichrysum (licorice plant 'Icicles')
Filler | ✿ ✿

Potted Pyramid

SEASON: Summer

LIGHT: ☼   **WATER:** ⬤

DESCRIPTION:

When I take a close look into the blooms of lantana 'Bandana Cherry', I'm amazed by the complexity of colours in just one flower: hints of coral, peach, pink, and even red. That palette spills over in the blooms of Diascia 'Diamonte Coral Rose', the delicate pink blooms of Gaura, and the burgundy blades of cordyline 'Red Star'. The natural shape of the plants in this combination forms the ultimate potted pyramid.

TIPS AND TRICKS:

- Gaura is an underused and misunderstood plant. With dainty flowers set on pink spikes, it's easily overlooked if planted alone in the garden, but in mass plantings it offers great height and colourful displays. In a pot like this one, Gaura is an ideal filler, offering unique texture and a fine surprise of small flowers pushed up through the foliage.
- Cordyline and lantana can be treated as patio tropicals and brought indoors in fall, but remove the Diascia and Gaura from the container and discard them at the end of the season.

Gaura ('Passionate Rainbow')
Filler | ✿✿

Diascia ('Diamonte Coral Rose')
Spiller | ✿✿✿

Lantana
('Bandana Cherry')
Filler | ✿✿

ordyline ('Red Star')
Thriller | ✿

Breezy Blooms

SEASON: Summer

LIGHT: ☼   **WATER:** 💧💧

DESCRIPTION:

The sturdy stems of perennial coneflower in this combination are the perfect complement to the fabulous foliage of Persian shield. The flowers of purple salvia partner well with 'Mini Dragon Wing' begonias (a new variety); the contrasting colours of verbena 'Lascar Dark Blue' and the magenta million bells spill over the edge. But the real thriller in this combination is not a plant at all—it's the wonderful whirling sunflower accessories that come alive in the breeze and boast flowers that are certain to last for years.

TIPS AND TRICKS:

- The purple sunflower whirligig in this container doesn't exactly create a refined look, but it will bring a smile to every child and child-at-heart who sees it. Don't be afraid to add fun accessories to some of your planters— they're great performers that require no effort, no water, and no fertilizer.
- Echinacea 'Lilliput' is a perennial and can be salvaged in the fall, but everything else in this mix can be enjoyed for one season only.

Echinacea (coneflower 'Lilliput')
Thriller | ✿

Strobilanthes (Persian shield)
Filler | ✿

Begonia ('Mini Dragon Wing' pink)
Filler | ✿

Calibrachoa (million bells 'MiniFamous Double Magenta')
Spiller | ✿✿✿

Salvia (purple)
Filler | ✿✿

Verbena ('Lascar Dark Blue')
Spiller | ✿✿

Summer

Water
Wise

Succulent Summer

SEASON: Summer/Fall

LIGHT: ☼ **WATER:** ◊

DESCRIPTION:

Sedum is a versatile, hardy perennial that comes in many varieties, all with fantastic foliage. While all of the sedum listed here are technically both sedum and stonecrops, you'll often hear "stonecrop" used to refer to plants with a trailing habit, whereas upright plants are referred to as sedum. The silvery grey 'Autumn Joy' provides the substance here; the burgundy stems of 'Bon Bon', the lemony foliage of 'Gold Moss', and the beautiful blooms of annual purslane add the colour. This simple collection of foliage will create endless summer interest; then the stonecrops will bloom and reward you again.

TIPS AND TRICKS:

- This is the ultimate combination for the water-wise. Stonecrop and purslane are succulents, which means they store a lot of water in their leaves and can survive the hottest and driest days. They perform best when planted in poor soils, so I like to use a potting mix of one-third sand to increase drainage.
- I wouldn't be surprised if this container survived on just rainfall, without fertilizer. But for peak performance, water it occasionally and fertilize it once in midsummer.
- I've had great success overwintering stonecrop in a pot. 'Gold Moss' will even seed itself easily, making a great ground cover. I once planted it in a container that was set on large river stones. Not only did it survive the winter, but the following spring its seeds germinated in the spaces between the stones.

Sedum
(stonecrop 'Gold Moss')
Spiller | ✿

Sedum
(stonecrop 'Lemon Coral')
Spiller | ✿

Sedum
(stonecrop 'Autumn Joy')
Thriller | ✿

Sedum
(stonecrop 'Bon Bon')
Thriller/Filler | ✿

Portulaca (purslane mixed)
Spiller | ✿

Summer

Red Rust

SEASON: Summer

LIGHT: ☼   **WATER:** 💧💧

DESCRIPTION:

Barberry is a traditional landscaping shrub that rarely ends up in a pot. But I chose it for this combo because it's an ideal thriller for the red/rust colour theme. With spotted leaves of red to pink to white, 'Rose Glow' combines perfectly with the popping orange blooms of New Guinea (or sunshine) impatiens, the red trumpet-shaped flowers of 'Potunia', and the rusty foliage of 'Sweet Caroline Bronze' potato vine.

TIPS AND TRICKS:

- You can try overwintering 'Rose Glow' in the pot, though you will improve your chances of success by moving it to the garden or by placing the whole container in the ground. If it works, you won't have to pot it again next season.
- Potato vine 'Sweet Caroline Bronze' will need the occasional pinching to keep it from dominating. Cut the 'Potunia' back by half in summer (or whenever it appears tired) to encourage fresh growth later in the season.
- Deadhead the impatiens and remove dead or decaying foliage from all of the plants to keeps the container clean and free of disease.

New Guinea impatiens (orange)
Filler | ✿ ✿

Petunia ('Potunia' red)
Spiller | ✿ ✿

Barberry ('Rose Glow')
Thriller | ✿

Sweet potato vine
(ipomoea 'Sweet Caroline Bronze')
Spiller | ✿ ✿

 **Summer**

Take Me to Tuscany

SEASON: Summer

LIGHT: ☼   **WATER:** 💧

DESCRIPTION:

Whenever I see this container I think of the balconies of Tuscany. Even with such a simple two-plant mix, this container makes quite a dramatic statement. Three 'Deep Red' geraniums fill the pot and add height, while the Scaevola drooping from the base of the geraniums softens the look and adds movement. Take this planter to a sunny corner of your yard, keep it well watered, and you can enjoy this bit of Europe all summer. *Viva Italia!*

TIPS AND TRICKS:

- To keep this container looking spectacular, regular fertilizer is a must, as geraniums are heavy feeders. Remove all spent flowers to encourage new ones. Deadheading geraniums can be tricky and sticky, so grab your scissors to make this a quick and tidy job.
- For a traditional Italian look, use a terracotta pot—you can even plant this mix in several terracotta pots of various sizes. If you use real clay pots, empty the container before the winter comes or it may end up in three or four pieces when it freezes. You can now buy plastic and fibreglass pots that look like clay but are much more durable.

Scaevola (white)
Spiller | ✿ ✿ ✿

Geranium ('Caliente Deep Red')
Thriller/Filler | ✿ ✿ ✿

Summer

100% Edible

Simply Salad

SEASON: Summer

LIGHT: ☼   **WATER:** 💧💧

DESCRIPTION:

Imagine asking your guests to choose their own salad greens! This container will be a conversation piece at any gathering. It's sweet peas with a common mixture of lettuce and other edible greens that you plant from seed. The arugula (which has gone to seed in the photo) provides the natural thriller, rising above the varieties in this unique mix. Leaf lettuce, Boston, romaine, and purple radicchio fill the pot, and sweet peas topple out the front. Pass the olive oil!

TIPS AND TRICKS:

- A small family could eat salad for the entire summer from a container of this size. Harvest the greens by cutting them to within about 5 cm (2 inches) of the soil—they'll grow back for a second (and maybe a third and fourth) harvest. This container looks its best before anything is harvested, so that's the time to have visitors.
- Later in the season, when the greens are not at their best, the sweet peas will bloom, adding vibrant colour.

Sweet pea
Spiller | ● ● ● ●

Mesclun ('Simply Salad')
Thriller/Filler | 2 seed packs

Puttin' on the Ritz

SEASON: Summer

LIGHT: ☼   **WATER:** 💧💧

DESCRIPTION:

I bought a pinstripe suit before planting this container, and I was inspired to include the brand new 'Pinstripe' variety of petunia. Then I decided to add the white Chilean potato vine (this one is a standard, which means it's been pruned upright) as a kind of top hat. The colours of both the dainty double Marguerite daisies and the cascading million bells can be found in the stripe of the petunia, which graduates from the palest pink to a shade of deep, dark purple.

TIPS AND TRICKS:

- Marguerite daisies, with their soft fern-like leaves, are annuals that bloom all summer. They're now available in shades of yellow, pink, and white. To encourage continuous colour, remove the spent flowers.
- 'Pinstripe' petunia is a fabulous variety that was introduced in 2011. It will continue to bloom all season long without deadheading.

Chilean potato vine (white)
Thriller | ❁

Petunia ('Pinstripe')
Spiller | ❁ ❁

Argyranthemum
(Marguerite daisy 'Molimba Helio Double Pink')
Filler | ❁ ❁ ❁

Calibrachoa (million bells blue)
Spiller | ❁ ❁

Strawberry-Rhubarb Pie

SEASON: Summer

LIGHT: ☼ **WATER:** 💧💧

DESCRIPTION:

Imagine waking up on a summer morning and stepping outside your door to pick fresh berries for your cereal. Red currant and blueberry give this container height, while an ever-bearing strawberry trails from the pot with a sprinkling of fruit and flowers. The large leaves and brilliant red stems of the rhubarb complete the look. Pie anyone?

TIPS AND TRICKS:

- When we talk about edible containers, people often immediately think of vegetables, but fruit is a beautiful and delicious option—just get playful with your combination. This container makes a great gift for a new homeowner. It can be enjoyed on the patio for the summer and then transplanted in the garden in the fall.
- Be careful if you have children or pets: rhubarb stems are delicious, but the leaves of this plant are highly toxic.

Red currant
Thriller | ✿

Rhubarb ('Canada Red')
Filler/Spiller | ✿

Strawberry
('Pretty in Pink')
Spiller | ✿ ✿

Blueberry ('Spartan')
Thriller | ✿

Night Light

New Guinea impatiens (white)
Filler | ❀ ❀ ❀

SEASON: Summer

LIGHT: ☼   **WATER:** 💧💧

DESCRIPTION:
Petunias as black as night intermingle with stark white lobelia and million bells in this dramatic container. Sparkling white geraniums and New Guinea impatiens (often called sunshine impatiens) shine at the top; the grey licorice plant fills in the gaps. This planter is guaranteed to bloom all season—it just keeps getting bigger and bolder as the weeks go by.

Petunia ('Black Velvet')
Spiller | ❀ ❀ ❀ ❀

TIPS AND TRICKS:
- This planter uses old-fashioned, tried-and-true plants, but it gets a contemporary makeover thanks to the black and white colour theme and the addition of the new 'Black Velvet' petunia.
- Using white plants in your containers brings them to life at night, when they are more visible than other colours. If you entertain in the evenings and want to draw attention to a certain part of the garden, this is your planter.

Lobelia ('Hot White')
Spiller | ❀ ❀ ❀

Helichrysum (licorice plant)
Spiller | ❀ ❀

Geranium (white)
Thriller/Filler | ❀

Calibrachoa (million bells white)
Spiller | ❀ ❀ ❀

Grandma's Quilt

SEASON: Summer

LIGHT: ☼   **WATER:** 💧💧

DESCRIPTION:

The pink, yellow, purple, and blue of this combination remind me of the floral prints on the kind of quilt a grandma would wrap around a child on a cool summer evening. The tiny blooms of Bidens, bacopa, and million bells form the background for the purple-veined 'Sugar Daddy' petunia that spills out of the container. The airy blooms of the cleome contrast beautifully with the dark foliage of the 'Black Lace' elderberry. And barely visible among this abundance of flowers is a single pink geranium.

TIPS AND TRICKS:

- This container is very overplanted—but look at the lush results. You should always plant your containers closer than you would in the garden. If one plant does not thrive, there will be another close by to take its place, and your planter will always look full.
- If this container gets leggy, cut back the petunia, the Bidens, and the million bells by about half. You'll be rewarded with a flush of new growth later in the season.
- Deadhead the cleome and geraniums regularly.

Cleome (purple)
Thriller/Filler | ✿✿

Geranium (pink)
Filler | ✿

Petunia ('Sugar Daddy')
Spiller | ✿✿

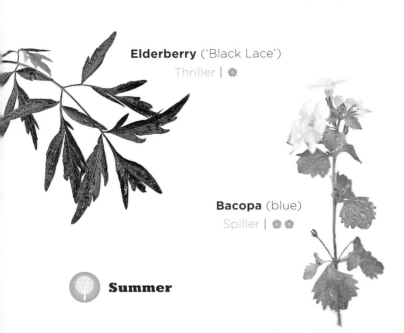

Elderberry ('Black Lace')
Thriller | ✿

Bacopa (blue)
Spiller | ✿✿

Calibrachoa (million bells pink with yellow centre)
Spiller | ✿✿

Bidens (yellow)
Spiller | ✿✿✿

Hat Trick

SEASON: Summer

LIGHT: ☼   **WATER:** ♦♦

DESCRIPTION:

String together three goals and you've got a hat trick; combine three great plants and you've got this fantastic container. Geranium, lobelia, and Scaevola make a winning trio. The bold red geraniums with variegated leaves will take no time at all to bulk up this container, and the hardy Scaevola billows out the bottom in periwinkle blue. White lobelia fills in any spaces left on the sides and complements the blue of the Scaevola.

Lobelia ('Hot White')
Spiller | ❀ ❀

TIPS AND TRICKS:

- This is a tough combination that can withstand a hot, sunny location. The lobelia will be protected from the hot rays of the sun by the foliage of the other plants, and by the time it burns out, the rest of the container will be so full it won't be missed.
- Scaevola will continue to bloom all summer without deadheading, although if it gets too gangly, you may want to pinch it back. As long as you remove the spent flowers of the geraniums, they'll continue to produce more blooms all season.
- To keep this container vibrant, fertilize every 10 days.

Geranium (variegated red)
Thriller/Filler | ❀ ❀

Scaevola ('Surdiva Blue')
Spiller | ❀ ❀

California Dreaming

SEASON: Summer

LIGHT: ☼   **WATER:** 💧💧

DESCRIPTION:
The centre of interest in this container is oleander, a popular patio tropical. You'll see oleander on the roadsides of southern California, where it gets abused but still produces beautiful five-petalled flowers all summer long. The fantastic foliage of 'Chocolate Mint' coleus and both dark and light pink Rieger begonias fill the base of the pot; purple million bells spill their blooms right to the floor. Easy to grow, with a diversity of foliage, flower size, and colour, this is a combination that dreams are made of—California dreams, that is!

TIPS AND TRICKS:
- The oleander in this combo is in standard form (pruned to grow upright) and will need to be staked early in the season or it may get uprooted. Within a month, the plant will root itself in the pot.
- Oleander can be brought inside before the risk of frost in late fall and over-wintered indoors. A warning: oleander is poisonous, so avoid it if you have pets or children who enjoy chewing plants.
- Deadheading the begonias will reduce the chances of rotting and promote strong growth with far more blooms.
- Depending on the light, the purple million bells will appear purple to complement the coleus, or almost pink to complement the begonias, as they do here. It's two plants in one!

Rieger begonia (dark pink)
Filler/Spiller | ✿ ✿

Rieger begonia (light pink)
Filler/Spiller | ✿

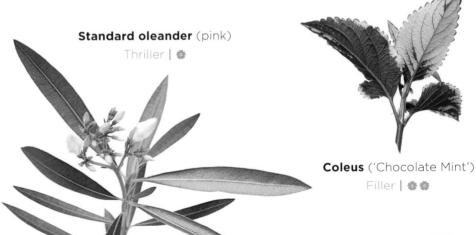

Standard oleander (pink)
Thriller | ✿

Calibrachoa
(million bells purple)
Spiller | ✿ ✿

Coleus ('Chocolate Mint')
Filler | ✿ ✿

Summer

Vibrant Visions

SEASON: Summer

LIGHT: ☼   **WATER:** ◐◐

DESCRIPTION:
This explosion of colour is not recommended for small spaces. The glossy green leaves of the hibiscus help the bright pink blooms pop out above a collection of brightly coloured double geraniums and a carpet of yellow and pink million bells. Give this container lots of room and watch it grow.

TIPS AND TRICKS:
- This sun-loving combination is fuss free for novice growers. Geraniums and hibiscus are forgiving of forgetful waterers, as both are resistant to drought. Just don't neglect watering altogether.
- All the care this container needs is some occasional deadheading of the geraniums and hibiscus. A single late-summer pinching of the million bells will keep their colour flowing right up until frost.

Calibrachoa (million bells pink)
Spiller | ✿✿

Hibiscus
(pink with red centre)
Thriller | ✿

Double geranium (red)
Filler | ✿✿

Calibrachoa (million bells yellow)
Spiller | ✿✿

 **Summer**

Low
Maintenance

Poker Face

SEASON: Summer

LIGHT: ☼   **WATER:** 💧💧

DESCRIPTION:
The stately upright stalks of red hot poker 'Flamenco' look like torches, with a collection of sun-loving plants basking in their glow. The heat continues with drought-tolerant plantings of 'Angelina' stonecrop and 'Moonbeam' coreopsis, surrounded by the dependable blooms of red, yellow, and orange marigolds.

TIPS AND TRICKS:
- This is a mix of four really easy plants. Red hot poker (also called torch lily), stonecrop, coreopsis, and marigolds are all known for being low maintenance as well as colourful—a great combination. A little deadheading of the red hot poker and marigolds is all the maintenance this container needs.
- During extended periods of wet weather, drainage is essential. Don't let these plants sit in water for prolonged periods or you risk root rot.

African marigold (orange)
Filler | ❀ ❀ ❀

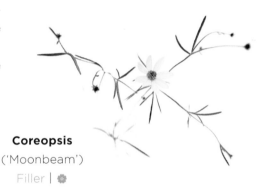

Coreopsis
('Moonbeam')
Filler | ❀

Marigold ('Durango Red')
Filler | ❀ ❀ ❀ ❀ ❀

Sedum
(stonecrop 'Angelina')
Spiller | ❀ ❀ ❀

Marigold
('Durango Yellow')
Filler | ❀ ❀ ❀

Red hot poker
('Flamenco')
Thriller | ❀

Summer

Traditional Twist

SEASON: Summer

LIGHT: ☼   **WATER:** 🌢🌢

DESCRIPTION:

Here's a combination with a traditional thrill but an upgraded spill and fill. The familiar dracaena spikes get a new look by being partnered with the stunning black and yellow blooms of 'Pinstripe' petunia, along with dark pink geraniums and the stunning foliage of 'Shining Sunsation' weigela.

TIPS AND TRICKS:

- I like taking traditional container plants like dracaena and evolving their look by adding new plant varieties. 'Pinstripe' is a just-introduced petunia hybrid, and 'Shining Sunsation' is a new variety of weigela. "Something old, something new" is a no-fail motto.
- Deadhead the geraniums and pinch the petunias in late summer to prolong their bloom time.

Petunia ('Pinstripe')
Spiller | ✿ ✿ ✿

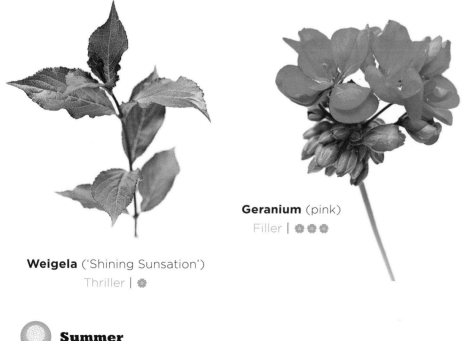

Weigela ('Shining Sunsation')
Thriller | ✿

Geranium (pink)
Filler | ✿ ✿ ✿

Dracaena
Thriller/Filler | ✿

Prickly Trickle

SEASON: Summer

LIGHT: ☼   **WATER:** ⬥

DESCRIPTION:

Wild and whimsical, soft yet prickly, cool and comforting—just a few words that describe this container of unique textures and blue blooms. 'Big Blue' sea holly is a stunning plant with thistle-like foliage, spiky stems, and silvery blue flowers. Beneath it, the blooms of Scaevola resemble water trickling to the ground. The needle-like foliage of the agave adds to the desert feel of this drought-tolerant planter, which will make the warmest spaces feel cooler on a summer day.

TIPS AND TRICKS:

- Sometimes a container can create a mood in a surprising way. The plants in this container love the heat, but their monochromatic blue colour theme creates the impression of coolness.
- Keep this container watered regularly, but don't fertilize more than once a month.

Agave
Filler | ✿ ✿ ✿

Scaevola (blue)
Spiller | ✿ ✿ ✿

Eryngium
(sea holly 'Big Blue')
Thriller | ✿

Nevada Sun

SEASON: Summer

LIGHT: ☼   **WATER:** ♦

DESCRIPTION:

Are you away during most weekends in the summer? If so, selecting drought-tolerant plants will allow you to get away with a few days of missed waterings. This combination of succulents and heat-loving tropical plants is strong enough to survive the hottest, driest days. The spiky blades of yucca make me think of the Nevada desert—it's in the same family as the famous Joshua trees of the American Southwest. The fleshy red 'Sanford's' hens and chicks contrast wonderfully with the bluish green succulent stems of 'Blue Spruce' stonecrop.

TIPS AND TRICKS:

- Succulent plants like stonecrop and hens and chicks retain water, and like cactuses they can survive extended periods of drought. The key to helping these plants thrive is to allow them to dry out completely between waterings. Adding some sand (about one-fifth of the overall volume) into the potting soil helps increase drainage. You could even use a potting soil designed for cactuses.
- Water this container only when it is thoroughly dry, and fertilize only twice during the growing season.
- Stonecrop and hens and chicks are perennials. Not only can they be salvaged for the garden but they'll even overwinter in a container. Yucca is a tropical and will need to be brought indoors before frost.

Yucca
Thriller | ✿

Sedum
(stonecrop 'Blue Spruce')
Spiller | ✿

Hens and chicks
('Sanford's')
Filler | ✿ ✿

Summer

Mexicana

SEASON: Summer

LIGHT: ☼   **WATER:** 💧💧

DESCRIPTION:

With tropical plants and *muy caliente* colours, this container is like a Mexican fiesta that will bloom all summer long. The red cordyline spikes and the glossy leaves of 'Janet Craig' dracaena complement each other; the bright blooms of the geraniums and strawflowers bring some sizzle. Meanwhile, the trailing foliage of potato vine adds a splash of lime to your margarita!

TIPS AND TRICKS:

- I enjoy using plant combinations that give clues to who lives in the home. If you have children, strawflowers are ideal. The blooms have the appearance of dried flowers (in fact, they're often grown for dried arrangements), and they'll grab the attention of any child with their colour and texture.
- Keep the party going all season by frequently deadheading the geraniums and the strawflowers.

Cordyline
Thriller | ❁

Geranium ('Tango Orange')
Filler | ❁ ❁

Dracaena ('Janet Craig')
Filler | ❁

Bracteantha (strawflower)
Filler | ❁ ❁ ❁

Sweet potato vine
(ipomoea lime)
Spiller | ❁ ❁ ❁

 **Summer**

Summer Heat

SEASON: Summer

LIGHT: ☼   **WATER:** 💧💧

DESCRIPTION:

Lemon yellow and lime green—a combination that says summer. The centrepiece of this super-simple container is a short standard hibiscus with bright yellow double flowers. It gets a lift from the lime-green potato vine that surrounds its base and spills out the side.

TIPS AND TRICKS:

- Hibiscus adds a tropical look to any container or garden. This plant thrives in the heat, but give it lots of water and weekly fertilizer when it's in bloom. Do not transplant a newly purchased hibiscus into too large a pot; this plant performs best when it is slightly root-bound, as long as there is adequate drainage.
- You can bring your hibiscus indoors in fall. Find a sunny location and cut back on water. Although it will not look great all winter (unless you have a greenhouse), your plant will come back to life next spring, even bigger and better than before.

Loves It Hot!

Standard hibiscus (yellow)
Thriller | ✿

Sweet potato vine (ipomoea lime)
Spiller | ✿✿✿

Summer

Mystic Spires

SEASON: Summer

LIGHT: ☼   **WATER:** ♦♦

DESCRIPTION:

This is a gorgeous combination, filled to overflowing with bright colours that will attract butterflies and hummingbirds to your deck. The hot pink of the geraniums in the front is repeated in both the flowers of the New Guinea (or sunshine) impatiens and the blades of the fountain grass. The tall salvia's deep blue flowers contrast perfectly as they reach to the sky.

TIPS AND TRICKS:

- 'Mystic Spires Blue' salvia is a winning choice for a thriller plant. It grows 30 to 36 cm (12 to 14 inches) tall, has beautiful purplish blue flowers that bloom all summer, and is drought tolerant to boot.
- The rest of this container is low maintenance too: both the geraniums and the fountain grass can take the heat of full sun and dry conditions. The geraniums will need to be deadheaded to encourage continuous blooms.

New Guinea impatiens (pink)
Filler | ❀❀❀❀

Pink fountain grass
Filler | ❀

Geranium
('Caliente' pink)
Filler/Spiller | ❀❀❀❀

Salvia
('Mystic Spires Blue')
Thriller | ❀❀❀

Attracts
Butterflies

Come to My Garden

SEASON: Summer

LIGHT: ☼   **WATER:** ♦

DESCRIPTION:

Not only is this container itself beautiful but it draws beauty to it. With the feathery liatris waving in the breeze, this planter looks inviting—to butterflies! The tiny red blooms of the pentas, the yarrow, and the stately purple coneflower—all are attractive to these creatures.

TIPS AND TRICKS:

- Butterfly gardening has become popular, and this planter is a good introduction to the hobby. Parsley is a common host plant for caterpillars, while all of the flowers provide nectar for adult butterflies. Keep this container in a sunny spot with water nearby, and enjoy the visitors.
- Liatris, commonly known as gayfeather, is an attractive upright perennial that is easy to grow and loves the heat. It reaches 120 cm (4 feet) and blooms in midsummer. The flowers are light purple or white.

Fernleaf yarrow
Filler | ❁ ❁

Liatris
Thriller | ❁ ❁ ❁ ❁

Pentas (red)
Spiller | ❁ ❁ ❁ ❁ ❁

Echinacea
(coneflower 'Majesty' purple)
Filler | ❁

Italian parsley
Filler | ❁ ❁ ❁

Yew Light Up My Life

SEASON: Summer/Fall

LIGHT: ☼   **WATER:** ●●

DESCRIPTION:

The golden glow of sunburst yew makes this container look fresh as spring. Contrasting black petunias tumble out the side, making the clusters of blue ageratum look safe and snug in front. The yew in this combo has been trimmed to standard form and will grow to about 1 1/2 metres (5 feet). Plant two of these containers, to stand on either side of your front door.

TIPS AND TRICKS:

- The yew needs full sun if you want to get the most of the bright golden shade of its new growth.
- You can overwinter the yew in the pot, as long as it is protected from cold winds and changing temperatures that can dry it up. Wrap it with burlap and place it in a sheltered corner. Water it until freeze-up, and remember to water it in spring before you bring it out to enjoy.
- Ageratum is a summer flowering annual that stays low, so it's a good choice for containers, as well as in the front of a garden. It thrives in full sun but will also bloom in part shade.

Petunia ('Black Velvet')
Spiller | ✿ ✿ ✿ ✿

Ageratum (blue)
Filler | ✿ ✿ ✿ ✿ ✿ ✿ ✿ ✿

Sunburst yew
Thriller | ✿

Changing Colours

SEASON: Summer

LIGHT: ☼   **WATER:** 🌢🌢

DESCRIPTION:

There's a lot happening at both the top and bottom of this container. The rose colour of the barberry branches is picked up by the bold shade of the zinnias, which tower above the other fillers. The lacy foliage and dangling daisy-like fragrant flowers of Brachycome fall out in front of the torch-like blooms of the Celosia. Sandwiched between are the fan-shaped leaves of Karasuba, which add all-season interest. This is one container whose colours will keep you guessing.

TIPS AND TRICKS:

- Karasuba is a cool foliage plant that spreads well and makes a good ground cover. I used it in this container because the foliage will change over the summer: the leaves start off green and gradually turn red, beginning at the tips. By fall they will be a bright scarlet.
- The 'Rose Glow' barberry gets its name from the barbs that grow along its branches. In the spring, its leaves are whitish pink, blending into a deeper rose with green at the base. In autumn the colour changes to a hot red with brilliant red berries. Easy to grow, these shrubs should be planted in full sun to reach full colour.

Celosia (yellow)
Filler | ❁ ❁ ❁ ❁

Zinnia (pink)
Filler | ❁ ❁ ❁ ❁

Brachycome (blue)
Spiller | ❁ ❁ ❁ ❁

Karasuba ('Crimson Fans')
Filler | ❁ ❁

Barberry ('Rose Glow')
Thriller | ❁

Firecracker

SEASON: Summer

LIGHT: ☼   **WATER:** ♦♦

DESCRIPTION:

The huge bronze leaves of the canna look striking in this container—so imagine the impact when the blooms appear later in summer. This combo delivers a dazzling display of colour, from the blazing fire red of the salvia to the lime and red blend of the coleus, and will add a spot of vibrancy to your front door.

TIPS AND TRICKS:

- 'Red King Humbert' canna is not hardy in most of Canada, so its rhizome must be dug up and brought indoors to store for the winter. But the display it shows in the summer makes it worth the effort. As the rhizome grows, you can carefully separate it and grow multiple plants. Make sure each piece of the rhizome has three to five "eyes."
- Both coleus and impatiens are usually considered shade plants, but these varieties are exceptions. The leaves of 'Fireball' are a showy blend of burgundy and lime green. This variety of New Guinea impatiens (commonly called sunshine impatiens) also has variegated leaves in yellow and green, with a red vein. Keep both of these plants well watered.

New Guinea impatiens
(orange with variegated leaf)
Filler/Spiller | ✿✿✿

Coleus ('Fireball')
Filler/Spiller | ✿✿✿

Canna
('Red King Humbert')
Thriller | ✿

Salvia ('Red Vista')
Filler | ✿✿✿

Repels Mosquitoes

Go Away!

SEASON: Summer

LIGHT: ☼   **WATER:** 💧💧

DESCRIPTION:
Pretty as this container is, you may be the only one who is attracted to it. I had some fun with this combo, mixing several different plants that are natural repellents. The citrosa at the top is said to discourage mosquitoes, and the brightly coloured marigolds are my favourite way to repel aphids, beetles, and whiteflies from the vegetable garden. The spiller is rue, a perennial with a scent that cats dislike.

TIPS AND TRICKS:
- There's a lot of controversy about the mosquito-repellent abilities of citrosa. Experts say this plant will do nothing to repel the pests when it's sitting in a pot, but if you crush its leaves they supposedly have the power of 40 per cent DEET. Fine, but who wants to crush the leaves?
- Rue can reach over 60 cm (2 feet) high in full sun and will keep cats out of any area it grows. In fact, you can dry and crush the leaves and sprinkle them in pots of houseplants or outdoor containers to keep cats out.

Marigold (bicolour)
Filler | ✿✿✿✿

Rue
Spiller | ✿✿✿

Marigold (orange)
Filler | ✿✿

Citrosa
Thriller | ✿✿✿

Pink Plaid

SEASON: Summer

LIGHT: ☼☀ **WATER:** 💧💧

DESCRIPTION:

This plant mixture was inspired by Pink Tartan, Canadian designer Kimberley Newport-Mimran's smart, sophisticated line of clothing, which is one of my wife's favourites. It uses a core of soft pink colours, complemented by dark foliage and a multitude of textures. With a whimsical yet refined feel, the combination extends a welcome and leaves a lasting impression—the way Laurie does with me.

TIPS AND TRICKS:

- This is an ideal container mix for a low-maintenance garden. All you need to do is occasionally deadhead the geraniums, Scaevola, and coral bells and remove any tired growth on the Pennisetum. In late summer pinch back the Scaevola to stimulate new growth.

Geranium ('Caliente' pink)
Filler | ❀❀

Scaevola (pink)
Spiller | ❀❀❀

Heuchera
(coral bells 'Shanghai')
Filler | ❀

Pennisetum ('Fireworks')
Thriller/Filler | ❀

Big Bean

SEASON: Summer

LIGHT: ☼☼   **WATER:** 💧💧

DESCRIPTION:

Fast-growing castor bean creates a dramatic display with very little effort. With huge leaves and a stately structure, this thriller creates a lot of shade for the plants underneath, and an opportunity to create contrast with the caladium. Meanwhile, the Diascia, lantana, and double impatiens add a subtle punch of colour. The result is big in size, big in colour, and huge in overall impact.

TIPS AND TRICKS:

- Thrillers with large leaves can shade out fillers and spillers, creating a challenge but also an opportunity. The challenge is creating a mix that will survive while the plants fight over space, light, and moisture. The opportunity is the chance to grow shade-loving plants in a sunny location.
- Try to avoid placing this container in a windy location. If you have no choice, weigh down the pot.
- Due to the sheer size of the castor bean, regular watering and fertilizing is a must. You may want to apply a slow-release fertilizer when you plant this combo to make sure the plants get fed all season.
- A word of warning: castor bean seeds are toxic, so this is not a combo for those with young children.

Impatiens
('Double Fiesta Stardust Salmon')
Filler | ❁ ❁ ❁

Caladium (red)
Filler | ❁

Diascia ('Diamonte Coral Rose')
Spiller | ❁ ❁ ❁

Lantana ('Confetti')
Filler | ❁ ❁

Castor bean
Thriller | ❁

Summer

Carrot Sticks

SEASON: Summer/Fall

LIGHT: ☼◑ **WATER:** ♦♦

DESCRIPTION:

Here's a fun play on an edible combination. 'Bright Lights' Swiss chard is one of my favourite edible thrillers, with lush, colourful leaves and bright stems. The texture of Greek oregano's foliage and seed heads contrasts nicely with the chunky leaves of the Swiss chard, while the colours are complemented by the Diascia flowers and the foliage of the bloodleaf. As a finishing touch, I added carrot sticks to punch up the colour and create a culinary delight for the eyes. Just make sure you have supper ready for your guests when they arrive.

Diascia (coral)
Filler/Spiller | ✿✿

TIPS AND TRICKS:

- This combo was lacking colour before our photo shoot, but I came up with a quick and quirky solution. After a trip to the kitchen to grab a bag of carrots, this container went from lame to fame. You can always use a trick like this if you're having guests and you want to create a bit of a "yak factor." The carrots should last about a week outdoors—unless you have rabbits!

- Whether in a container or a garden bed, Swiss chard is awesome. It's colourful and good to eat, and frost tolerant to boot. The key to keeping it growing during the season is regular harvesting. Never fear: harvesting will promote fresh, new growth.

- Greek oregano enjoys regular harvesting too—it is fast growing and will return quickly after an occasional cut. However, to make this container look its best, let the flower heads and seed pods develop.

- Diascia and bloodleaf will meet their demise with cooler fall temperatures, but Swiss chard and oregano will keep performing. In fact, the colours of 'Bright Lights' will intensify.

Greek oregano
Filler | ✿✿✿

Iresine (bloodleaf)
Filler | ✿✿✿

Swiss chard
('Bright Lights')
Filler | ✿✿✿

Summer

Attracts
Hummingbirds

Calm and Cool

SEASON: Summer

LIGHT: ☼☼   **WATER:** 💧💧

DESCRIPTION:

Colour can have a genuine effect on moods: blues, whites, pinks, and pastels help to calm the spirit. As well, they can help to make smaller spaces feel larger. Blue salvia, plum million bells, and purple Angelonia—all contrasting with the white flowers of 'Wave' petunias and cleome—create a container that will add serenity to even the most chaotic of settings.

TIPS AND TRICKS:

- Overall this is a robust selection of plants that will do well during most summers. The only time you may see it struggle is during extended periods of extreme heat and humidity, but it will return to its former glory once temperatures cool off.
- The key to keeping this container looking cool and calm all season is deadheading. Cleome, salvia, Angelonia, and even the million bells need their spent blooms removed. If they aren't, disease may strike as the rotted flowers fall onto the foliage and the soil.
- Cleome is an annual that you'll rarely see in pots; rather, it's usually mass-planted in a garden. I feel that its height, its continual blooming period, and its interesting flower offer a unique element to any combination.

Petunia
('Easy Wave White Improved')
Spiller | ✿ ✿ ✿

Cleome ('Sparkler' white)
Filler | ✿ ✿ ✿ ✿

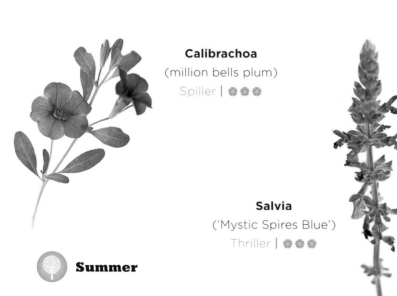

Calibrachoa
(million bells plum)
Spiller | ✿ ✿ ✿

Salvia
('Mystic Spires Blue')
Thriller | ✿ ✿ ✿

Angelonia (purple)
Filler | ✿ ✿ ✿

Summer

Hidden Nest

SEASON: Summer

LIGHT: ○◐ **WATER:** 💧💧

DESCRIPTION:

I have to be honest: I found this combination a little boring at first, since it has just two plant varieties. So I thought I would give it a bit of a "yak factor" by adding the metal swan, which looks like it's sitting on a nest hidden among the blooms. The heart-shaped, waxy leaves of 'Dragon Wing' begonia partner well with the euphorbia's foliage and dainty white blooms. Together this classic red and white combination would make an ideal tribute to Canada Day.

TIPS AND TRICKS:

- During the growing season you may get bored with your combinations. That's a sure sign of a true gardener—you're never satisfied with your results. You may be tempted to go out and buy some new plants, but I suggest you think of your container as an outfit. The pot is a combination of shoes and pants, while the plants are the shirt, with a choice of prints. Floral picks, trellises, and obelisks—or, in this case, a metal swan—are the accessories that will turn your combo into a memorable outfit. Like my wife says, an outfit is only as good as its accessories.
- 'Dragon Wing' begonia and euphorbia are care-free selections. Neither requires deadheading.

Euphorbia ('Breathless White')
Spiller | ❁ ❁ ❁

Begonia ('Dragon Wing' red)
Filler | ❁ ❁ ❁

Find the Lime

SEASON: Summer

LIGHT: ☼☼   **WATER:** 💧💧

DESCRIPTION:

This combination gets its name from the 'Lime Rickey' coral bells and the 'Lemon Star' black-eyed Susan. The combination of greens and yellows creates an inviting and soothing colour theme in this container. The chartreuse leaves of 'Lime Rickey' match perfectly with the airy look of Scotch moss, while contrasting against the deep green foliage of the black-eyed Susan. All of this provides a backdrop for the yellow blooms of the zinnia and strawflower.

TIPS AND TRICKS:

- During the growing season, taller plants tend to shade those beneath them. This container provides a good example: both the coral bells and the Scotch moss will eventually be overshadowed by the black-eyed Susan and the zinnia.
- Keep this pot looking good by deadheading the zinnias often and controlling the vigorous growth of the black-eyed Susan with regular trimming.

Zinnia ('Zahara' yellow)
Filler | ✿

Scotch moss
Filler/Spiller | ✿✿✿✿

Bracteantha
(strawflower yellow)
Thriller/Filler | ✿

Black-eyed Susan
('Lemon Star')
Thriller/Spiller | ✿✿

Heuchera
(coral bells 'Lime Rickey')
Filler | ✿

Sanvitalia ('Tsavo')
Filler | ✿✿

100% Edible

Lettuce Eat!

SEASON: Summer

LIGHT: ☼☼   **WATER:** 💧💧

DESCRIPTION:

This is a fun-looking container that would look inviting in front of a restaurant. Vegetables grown in pots look as delicious as they taste, and this combination of lettuce, endive, and celery creates a diversity of textures and conjures thoughts of a summer salad. To add to the theme of culinary delights, I've accessorized with a bowl of tomatoes that adds a much-needed punch of colour. This prop is also functional—you can use the bowl to toss your salad, tomatoes and all.

TIPS AND TRICKS:

- The leaf lettuce in the photo is past its prime for eating—I allowed it to go to seed instead of harvesting it. Growing up in Ontario's Holland Marsh, I often saw mature leaf lettuce with flowers and seed spikes and thought, "That's a cool plant!" I've tried to recreate that here.
- Although the lettuce is ready to harvest quickly, the celery is not. Growing celery in a pot is fun and it looks great, but it takes a long time to mature—it won't be ready until very late in the summer. Even then, don't expect it to have the big, thick stalks you'd see in a grocery store. Consider it an ornamental.
- When you cut the lettuce, leave about 5 cm (2 inches) above the soil. It should replenish itself in 7 to 10 days, giving you three to five harvests per season.

Endive
Filler | ✿ ✿ ✿

Lettuce ('Simpson Elite')
Filler | ✿ ✿

Celery
Filler | ✿

Red Rocket

SEASON: Summer

LIGHT: ☼ ☼   **WATER:** 💧💧

DESCRIPTION:

A perfect combination of flower, foliage, and texture, this container highlights the finest attributes of its three partners. Fuchsia 'Gartenmeister' rockets from the top of this planter with small, vibrant, trumpet-shaped flowers and dark foliage. 'Dragon Wing' begonia offers contrast with smooth waxed leaves and dainty, deep red blooms, while 'Double Magenta' million bells hide the soil and cascade over the rim.

TIPS AND TRICKS:

- When creating containers, why make things difficult? Here's an example of just three plants, each with its own strength. All three will bloom continuously through the summer.
- These plants are proven performers that grow without difficulty, as long as they have appropriate sunlight, regular watering, and occasional fertilizing. This combo will benefit from deadheading and pinching, but it will look good even if you forget.

Calibrachoa (million bells 'MiniFamous Double Magenta')
Spiller | ✿ ✿ ✿ ✿ ✿

Begonia ('Dragon Wing' red)
Filler | ✿ ✿ ✿

Fuchsia ('Gartenmeister')
Thriller | ✿ ✿

Frankie Favourite

Pink Perfection

SEASON: Summer

LIGHT: ☼☀   **WATER:** 💧💧

DESCRIPTION:
The inspiration for this container came from an old favourite that is often used indoors: 'Purple Heart' wandering Jew. Its dark wine-coloured leaves have a slight pink veining, which led me to partner it with variegated ornamental grass to continue the theme of bicoloured leaves. The pink veining of 'Purple Heart' also looks great alongside pink million bells and tuberous begonias, and against the backdrop of the dark elephant ear–like foliage of 'Black Magic' colocasia.

TIPS AND TRICKS:
- When choosing plants for a container, you should normally make sure they all have similar light requirements. In this case, however, I cheated a little. Tuberous begonia prefers part shade, but the thrillers in this combo will keep it out of the sun.
- Regular watering and occasional fertilizing are a must. To keep this container glowing until fall, cut back the million bells to promote fresh growth and remove the spent flowers of the tuberous begonia to reduce the chances of mould or disease.
- You can remove the colocasia tuber and store it in a cool, dark, dry place for planting next spring. 'Purple Heart' wandering Jew can be potted up and enjoyed indoors.

Calibrachoa (million bells pink)
Spiller | ✿✿✿

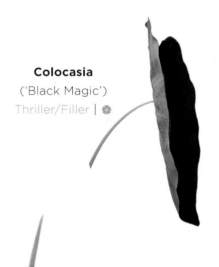

Colocasia
('Black Magic')
Thriller/Filler | ✿

Wandering Jew
('Purple Heart')
Filler | ✿✿

Tuberous begonia (pink)
Filler | ✿

Pennisetum ('Fireworks')
Thriller | ✿

Whimsical Wonder

SEASON: Summer

LIGHT: ☼☀ **WATER:** 🌢🌢

DESCRIPTION:

Okay, there's a lot going on in this planter—almost too much, I admit. But the complexity of this combination is what gives it interest. The arching stems of ornamental grasses, Angelonia, and not one but two varieties of lilyturf give the mix its height. The colour comes from the feather-like blooms of Celosia and the trailing trumpet flowers of the mauve million bells. This whimsical selection will create some magic in an otherwise quiet spot on a patio, porch, or terrace.

TIPS AND TRICKS:

- When a container is a little chaotic, like this one is, I like to add an anchor. Here I used the obelisk and mini glass ball to help draw the eye upward.
- Deadhead the Angelonia, lilyturf, and Celosia to stimulate additional flowering. A hard cutting back of the million bells in late summer will have this pot thriving well into fall.
- Regular watering and biweekly fertilizing are the only other maintenance this container needs.

Angelonia
('Angel Mist' deep plum)
Filler | ✿ ✿

Lobelia ('Techno Blue')
Spiller | ✿

Lilyturf (variegated)
Filler/Spiller | ✿

Hakone grass ('All Gold')
Thriller/Filler | ✿

Lilyturf
('Silver Dragon')
Filler/Spiller | ✿

Celosia (yellow)
Filler | ✿ ✿

Calibrachoa (millon bells mauve)
Spiller | ✿ ✿ ✿

Summer

Red Baron

SEASON: Summer

LIGHT: ☼ ☀   **WATER:** 💧💧

DESCRIPTION:

The steel crane accessory in this container appears to be in a natural marsh-like setting—except I've never seen a marsh this colourful. Hidden behind the red-tipped blades of Japanese blood grass, the bird seems to be looking at the vibrant blooms of the begonia, which partner well with the dark foliage of 'Bon Bon' stonecrop. The always awesome coleus 'Red Head' adds even more colour; the heart-shaped leaves of potato vine trail below. Never mind the flowers—based on foliage and fun, this combination will be the talk of the street.

TIPS AND TRICKS:

- The plants in this pot are colourful and creative, but it's the crane that really makes a statement. In fact, it was this accessory that guided my selections: I chose the grass to create a marsh-like scene and selected the other plants based on their complementary colours.
- Like every potato vine, 'Black Heart' is a vigorous grower. Pinch it back during the growing season to keep it from dominating your pot.
- Stonecrop is a hardy plant that can overwinter in a pot, but the others in this mix will need to be discarded in late fall.

Coleus ('Red Head')
Filler | ✿ ✿

Sweet potato vine
(ipomoea 'Black Heart')
Spiller | ✿ ✿

Japanese blood grass
('Red Baron')
Thriller | ✿ ✿

Sedum (stonecrop 'Bon Bon')
Thriller | ✿

Begonia
('Big Red with Bronze Leaf')
Filler/Spiller | ✿ ✿

Summer

Soft Serenity

SEASON: Summer

LIGHT: ☼◐ **WATER:** 💧💧

DESCRIPTION:

Green is good for the earth—and for the soul. This calming combo features four plants with different hues of green, as well as foliage with a variety of textures and sizes. The airy tufts of dwarf giant papyrus are underplanted with the soft mounding form of Irish moss, contrasting with the variegated heartleaf philodendron and the felt-like trailing foliage of licorice plant. This mix will help you create a feeling of serenity in any surrounding.

TIPS AND TRICKS:

- Colour is usually what people look for in gardening, but the real goal should be creating interest. This combination is a good example of how you can do that with texture, even with a monochromatic theme. Even the perched bird helps add to the peaceful setting.
- Irish moss is a perennial, but it's not likely to overwinter in a container—find a slightly shady spot for it in the garden. Papyrus and licorice plant won't survive another season either, but you can bring the philodendron indoors before the frost.
- Keep this container well watered, but you shouldn't need to fertilize more than once a month.

Cyperus (dwarf giant papyrus)
Thriller | ✿

Heartleaf philodendron
Filler/Spiller | ✿✿✿

Irish moss
Filler | ✿✿✿

Summer

227

Dark Chocolate

SEASON: Summer

LIGHT: ☼◐ **WATER:** ♦♦

DESCRIPTION:

Black is the new green in this exotic container. The huge leaves of 'Imperial Taro' offer a blend of green and black, while the mostly green foliage of coleus 'Chocolate Splash' has a dark splotch on each leaf. The blooms of 'Nonstop Mocca White' tuberous begonia spring from the dark background of its foliage, and the heart-shaped leaves of 'Blackie' sweet potato vine add the spill.

TIPS AND TRICKS:

- I love the richness of dark foliage, but if you overdo it, your container can become a black hole. Contrast is key. This mix achieves that with some bright green and a small planting of white blooms, though dark foliage also works well with pink, red, and orange.
- For even more dramatic contrast, plant this combination in a white container.
- Deadhead the begonias to prevent rotting and disease, and keep the sweet potato vine in check by pinching it back. You can increase the fullness of the coleus by pinching it once a month too.
- 'Imperial Taro' can be overwintered: remove its tuber in late fall and store it indoors in a cool, dark, dry place.

Sweet potato vine
(ipomoea 'Blackie')
Spiller | ❀❀

Tuberous begonia
('Nonstop Mocca White')
Spiller | ❀❀❀

Coleus ('Chocolate Splash')
Filler | ❀❀

Colocasia ('Imperial Taro')
Thriller | ❀

Pure Chardonnay

SEASON: Summer

LIGHT: ☼ ☀   **WATER:** ♦♦♦

DESCRIPTION:

There's nothing better than a crisp, cold glass of Chardonnay in summer, and the freshness and colour of that wine was the inspiration for this container. The thriller is the flowering shrub deutzia 'Chardonnay Pearls', which finds a perfect match in the blooms of Celosia 'Fresh Look Yellow' and 'Nonstop Mocca Yellow' begonias. All of this is underplanted with variegated lilyturf and golden creeping Jenny. The purple Angelonia is a nod to those who prefer red wine.

TIPS AND TRICKS:

- A lot of gardeners avoid using flowering shrubs in containers, but I think they should be embraced. Deutzia 'Chardonnay Pearls' has a lot going for it. Not only does it sport dainty white flowers and great foliage but you can plant it in the garden in fall.
- Creeping Jenny and Jacob's ladder also offer both summer interest and longevity as perennials, but the others in this mix can be discarded in late fall.
- To keep this container looking great, deadhead the Celosia and begonia regularly. As for the deutzia flowers, remove the stems and give the plant a light pruning. Keep an eye out for any dead or decaying foliage and remove it immediately.

Jacob's ladder
('Stairway to Heaven')
Filler | ✿

Deutzia ('Chardonnay Pearls')
Thriller | ✿

Lysimachia (creeping Jenny)
Spiller | ✿ ✿

Celosia
('Fresh Look Yellow')
Thriller | ✿

Angelonia (purple)
Filler | ✿

Lilyturf (variegated)
Filler | ✿

Tuberous begonia
('Nonstop Mocca Yellow')
Filler | ✿ ✿

Summer

Cypress Sizzle

SEASON: Summer

LIGHT: ☼☀   **WATER:** 💧💧

DESCRIPTION:

The unique foliage and branching of the yellow Hinoki cypress have a very Asian feel that reminds me of a bonsai tree. It adds height and drama to the colourful display of 'Freckles' coleus and the vigorous trailing habit of lime, 'Blackie', and bronze potato vine. The blend of colour, size, shape, form, and texture in this leafy combination makes for one sizzling container.

TIPS AND TRICKS:

- Instead of looking for a diverse selection of plants, look for a single plant that offers a lot of diversity. Potato vine is a great example: the number of new varieties is constantly increasing, offering a huge selection of leaf shape and colour. You can come up with new combinations every year.
- Water this container regularly, as the Hinoki cypress is susceptible to water loss.

Coleus ('Freckles')
Filler | ✿✿

Yellow Hinoki cypress
Thriller | ✿

Sweet potato vine
(ipomoea lime)
Spiller | ✿

Sweet potato vine
(ipomoea 'Sweet Caroline Bronze')
Spiller | ✿

Sweet potato vine
(ipomoea 'Blackie')
Spiller | ✿

Orange Heart

SEASON: Summer

LIGHT: ☼◐ **WATER:** 💧💧

DESCRIPTION:

The dark foliage of dwarf painted banana, 'Purple Heart' wandering Jew, and 'Blackie' sweet potato vine creates the backdrop for bright blooms of 'Nonstop Mocca Deep Orange' tuberous begonias and orange New Guinea impatiens (also called sunshine impatiens) as the showy stems and dainty star-like flowers of the wandering Jew spill at the side.

TIPS AND TRICKS:

- Windy locations do not suit any container with ornamental banana, as their large, soft leaves tear easily. Place this pot in a sheltered location, but make sure it still gets bright light.
- With regular water and fertilizer, this container will sizzle all season long. But the first sign of Jack Frost will send a shiver through these plants, and they'll soon end up in the compost pile.

Sweet potato vine
(ipomoea 'Blackie')
Spiller | ✿

New Guinea impatiens (orange)
Filler | ✿ ✿ ✿ ✿ ✿

Wandering Jew
('Purple Heart')
Filler/Spiller | ✿

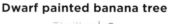

Dwarf painted banana tree
Thriller | ✿

Tuberous begonia
('Nonstop Mocca Deep Orange')
Filler | ✿ ✿ ✿

 **Summer**

Twist of Lime

SEASON: Summer

LIGHT: ☼◐ **WATER:** 💧💧

Sweet potato vine (ipomoea lime)
Spiller | ✿

DESCRIPTION:

Dwarf Alberta spruce is one of the few evergreens that can survive in the limited space of a container. In this combo, its soft lime-coloured new growth is reflected in the foliage of 'Faith' hosta and lime sweet potato vine, as well as the fantastic double blooms of 'Sweet Sunshine Compact Lime' petunia and even the star-like pattern within the flowers of 'Pinstripe' petunia. This container's mix of foliage and flowers, needles and leaves, and single and double blooms is cheerful and easy to care for.

Petunia ('Sweet Sunshine Compact Lime')
Spiller | ✿✿✿

TIPS AND TRICKS:

- Winter burn is a common threat to evergreens—moisture loss due to inadequate watering in fall, exposure to high winds, or strong sunshine can all cause evergreens to go brown. In a pot, winter burn happens even more often and can ultimately kill the plant. That's why I don't recommend trying to overwinter the dwarf Albert spruce in the container. However, if you want to keep it potted for next year, you can try burying the whole container in the soil. Keep it well watered until freeze-up.
- Keep this mix looking good by deadheading the double 'Sweet Sunshine Compact Lime' petunias and pinching back the potato vine occasionally.

Hosta ('Faith')
Filler | ✿

Petunia ('Pinstripe')
Spiller | ✿✿✿

Dwarf Alberta spruce
Thriller | ✿

Summer

Tropical Trails

SEASON: Summer

LIGHT: ☼☼   **WATER:** 💧💧

DESCRIPTION:

Buttercup blooms and dramatic height aren't the only thrills that the flowering senna has to offer. Its blue-green foliage also adds interesting form as it reaches down to touch the bright pink geraniums and the unique foliage of 'Freckles' coleus. Pink bacopa trail and spill over the container to complete the tropical feel.

TIPS AND TRICKS:

- This species of flowering senna is a vigorous tropical plant; in Florida and California it's often grown as a hedge. If you leave it unattended, it may become the bully in this combination. Prune it regularly to keep it in check and to encourage multiple buds and blooms.
- The combination of pink and yellow flowers may be dainty, but this is a tough container that will survive even if you occasionally forget to water it. Deadhead the geraniums and fertilize monthly to keep it performing well.

Coleus ('Freckles')
Filler | ✿

Geranium (pink)
Filler | ✿✿

Cassia (flowering senna yellow)
Thriller | ✿

Bacopa (pink)
Spiller | ✿✿

Summer

Preppy Pink

SEASON: Summer

LIGHT: ☼☀   **WATER:** 💧💧

DESCRIPTION:

This combination makes me think of the 1980s, with its buttoned-down Ralph Lauren shirts and "Brat Pack" movies. The lush foliage of both 'Kong Salmon Pink' and red leaf coleus contrasts fabulously with the double pink blooms of petunia and burgundy dahlia. The glossy leaves and bright red to pink buds of 'Dragon Wing' begonia add the thrill. Finally, the Rieger begonias add a knock-out punch to a container that looks pretty in pink.

TIPS AND TRICKS:

- Choosing a container combination doesn't have to be difficult. Just focus on one colour story and use that to drive your selections. In this case, my eye was drawn to the amazing foliage of 'Kong Salmon Pink' coleus. Its veined leaves of red, pink, and burgundy encouraged me to choose petunias, begonias, and a dahlia in similar shades.
- Deadhead the petunias and dahlia, and pinch the red leaf coleus to prevent it from growing too tall. Once-a-month fertilizer will also help keep this mix blooming.

Dahlia (burgundy)
Filler | ❀

Rieger begonia (pink)
Filler | ❀ ❀

Coleus
('Kong Salmon Pink')
Filler | ❀

Double petunia (pink)
Spiller | ❀ ❀ ❀

Begonia ('Dragon Wing' red)
Thriller | ❀

Red leaf coleus
Filler | ❀

100% Edible

Posh Spice

SEASON: Summer

LIGHT: ☼☀ **WATER:** 💧💧

DESCRIPTION:
Inspire your taste buds with this combination of savoury herbs that combines flavour, flowers, and foliage. The standard flowering basil is a towering thriller. Italian parsley and two varieties of sage spread around its base and the mounding magenta flowers of creeping thyme add the spill. Who knew herbs could look so good?

TIPS AND TRICKS:
- The standard basil I've used here may be hard to find at your local garden centre. You can substitute the more common columnar basil, which also has an upright growth habit.
- Use them or lose them. If you leave them unattended, most herbs will get leggy and appear weak. Regularly harvesting or pinching the basil, parsley, sage, and thyme will encourage healthy new growth.
- I like keeping herb planters like this close to my kitchen or barbecue area—the closer the herbs, the greater the chance they'll end up in my cooking.

Creeping thyme
Spiller | ✿

Sage (tri-colour)
Filler | ✿ ✿

Sage (traditional or common)
Filler | ✿ ✿ ✿

Standard flowering basil
Thriller | ✿

Italian parsley
Filler | ✿

Red Fox

SEASON: Summer

LIGHT: ☼☼   **WATER:** 💧💧

DESCRIPTION:

Here's a sun-loving container that will have you seeing red. The crimson blooms of the Mandevilla provide the thrill as the vine climbs up a trellis, while the glossy blooms of Anthurium fill the area beneath. The colour then continues with the foliage of red leaf coleus, and the fuzzy flowers of the foxtail spill over the edges to create a unique look.

TIPS AND TRICKS:

- Foxtail prefers part sun to shade, so you may wonder how it will survive in a container with sun worshippers. If the thriller and fillers in your combination are tall, they'll have the greatest exposure to sunlight and will provide some shelter for the trailing plants beneath, and that's the case here.
- Deadhead the foxtail, Anthurium, and Mandevilla. The Mandevilla will also need an occasional pruning, or a higher trellis, as it will grow beyond the reach of the one we've used here.

Mandevilla (red)
Thriller | ✿

Anthurium (red)
Filler | ✿

Chenille (foxtail)
Spiller | ✿✿

Red leaf coleus
Filler | ✿✿

Frankie Favourite

Banana Appeal

SEASON: Summer

LIGHT: ☼☼   **WATER:** ♦♦

DESCRIPTION:

With the lush leaves and copper stems of red leaf banana as the centrepiece, this container has a Central American feel that is well suited to a poolside or a tropical-themed garden or patio. The geraniums send up a constant stream of cherry-red flower heads, while the rex begonia and trailing flowers of pink million bells spill colour right to the floor.

TIPS AND TRICKS:

- Do not place this container in a windy location unless you like mashed banana. Even in sheltered locations, weigh down containers with tall thrillers by placing stones in the base of the pot when you do the planting.
- You'll need to deadhead the geraniums often. Although million bells tend to self-clean, I recommend a hard pruning (cut them back by half) in late summer to stimulate new growth right up until frost.

Rex begonia

Filler | ✿

Calibrachoa (million bells pink with red centre)

Spiller | ✿

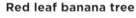

Red leaf banana tree

Thriller | ✿

Geranium (red)

Filler | ✿✿

 **Summer**

Icicles

SEASON: Summer

LIGHT: ☼☀   **WATER:** 💧

DESCRIPTION:

Here's a container that brings lots of movement to your space—even the slightest breeze will animate the blades of fountain grass and the silvery foliage of the lotus vine. The stems of the begonia and the fine oval leaves of the euphorbia pair up nicely in shades of pink and red. I especially love the way the licorice plant intermingles with the begonia blooms, making their pink appear even softer.

TIPS AND TRICKS:

- Lotus vine is a great filler or spiller in containers, hanging baskets, and window boxes. This low-maintenance plant is able to handle both heat and drought, and it's available in many varieties. It's a robust grower that can easily take over, however, so keep it under control by pinching it back.
- Wax begonias can tolerate the heat, so they're a favourite container plant for sun or shade. They flower in pink, white, or red from late spring to fall, and you can even bring them indoors.

Lotus vine (silver)
Spiller | ✿✿✿

Green fountain grass
Thriller | ✿

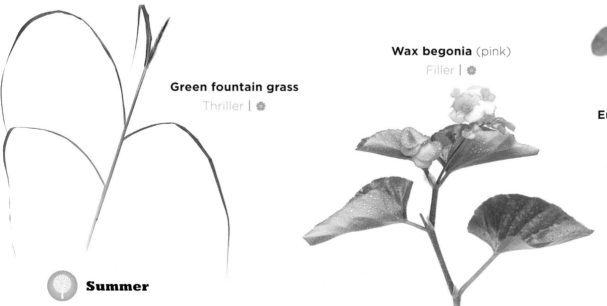

Wax begonia (pink)
Filler | ✿

Euphorbia (red)
Filler | ✿

Red Flare

SEASON: Summer

LIGHT: ○◑   **WATER:** 💧💧

DESCRIPTION:

Looking for a container that will be especially bold on a deck of dark wood? The spray of pink fountain grass is tinged with red, and it's surrounded by crimson spikes of salvia. The underplanting is a circle of dark leaf begonia that spills from the edge, with an accent of red and white petunias.

TIPS AND TRICKS:

- With its upright growth that spills out from the middle, fountain grass is a natural thriller. If you can't find the pink variety, look for others with bronze, purple, red, or green foliage. It does well in full to part sun and grows to up to 1 metre (3 feet).
- 'Dreams Red Picotee' is an upright variety of petunia, but it also spreads well and works as both a spiller and a filler with its showy red and white flowers. It will thrive in both sun and part shade.
- The begonias can withstand some hot sun throughout the day, but they do better in part sun.

Begonia
('Big Red with Bronze Leaf')
Filler/Spiller | ✿✿✿✿

Pink fountain grass
Thriller | ✿

Petunia ('Dreams Red Picotee')
Filler/Spiller | ✿✿✿✿

Salvia (red)
Filler | ✿✿✿✿

Summer

Romance

SEASON: Summer

LIGHT: ☼ ◐ **WATER:** 💧💧

DESCRIPTION:

Romance is complicated—and so is this container. The tiny flowers of the coral bells rise high above the other plants, and this movement is reflected by the trailing blooms of the lobelia below. A graceful red Asiatic lily competes with the dahlia for attention, while verbena dangles below. The fiery red theme is enhanced by the burgundy foliage of the cordyline on one side.

TIPS AND TRICKS:

- Verbena is very popular in containers and with good reason. It comes in a huge variety of colours: reds, pinks, purples, and white. It's drought tolerant and produces clusters of flowers on a plant that grows freely. By September the rest of this container will have fizzled like a summer romance, but the verbena will keep blooming until frost.

- This mix will produce continuous colour: the coral bells will bloom in late spring or early summer, and the Asiatic lily will follow with its rich red hues and wonderful fragrance. The dahlia and verbena will stay in bloom for the remainder of the summer.

- Both coral bells and Asiatic lily are perennials. Transplanting them in fall will give you many years of enjoyment.

Verbena (red)
Spiller | ✿

Lobelia ('Techno Blue')
Spiller | ✿✿

Asiatic lily ('Tiny Puppet')
Filler | ✿

Heuchera
(coral bells 'Sashay')
Thriller | ✿

Dahlia ('Figaro' red)
Filler | ✿✿✿

Cordyline
('Caruba Black')
Filler | ✿

🌳 **Summer**

Coleus Companions

SEASON: Summer

LIGHT: ☼☀   **WATER:** 💧💧

DESCRIPTION:

The whole palette of this container is showcased in the flowers and foliage of the 'Sunlover' coleus. The outline of the leaf matches the sunshine yellow of the double million bells, which fill out the front of the container and reach almost to the ground. The two shades of pink (which gradually fade to black) in the centre of the leaves are mirrored in the New Guinea impatiens (often called sunshine impatiens), and the fluttering fish-like bloom of the goldfish plant repeats these shades. Finally, the lime green shows up in the philodendron and really pops out among the dark foliage.

TIPS AND TRICKS:

- Coleus is a perfect starting point for picking a colour theme for any container. It's available in a wide range of colours, including burgundy, scarlet, watermelon, and lime. Pick up these colours in the other plants you choose and you can't go wrong.
- New varieties of coleus make this plant more versatile than ever. In the past, coleus was pretty much a shade lover, but now there are lots of varieties that can tolerate full sun. Just make sure you don't mix the two in the same container or you'll get one that thrives and one that fades. Create a beautiful echo of this container in your garden by placing some coleus in a corner with the right light conditions.

Coleus ('Sunlover')
Thriller/Filler | ❁❁

Goldfish plant
Thriller/Filler | ❁❁

Philodendron (yellow)
Filler | ❁❁❁

New Guinea impatiens
(pink and orange)
Filler | ❁❁❁

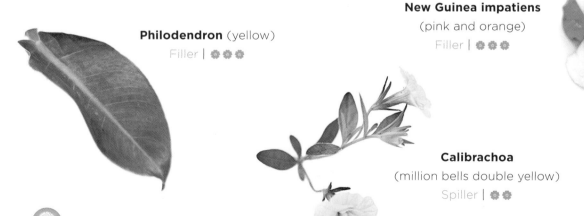

Calibrachoa
(million bells double yellow)
Spiller | ❁❁

Summer

Lemon Fizz

SEASON: Summer

LIGHT: ☼☀   **WATER:** 💧💧

DESCRIPTION:
Although this combo features just two colours, the variety of textures creates a lot of interest. Lemon yellow nemesia tumble over the sides, looking like the tiny offspring of the double rieger begonias behind them. Overhead, a fountain of Pennisetum showers down. A 'Janet Craig' dracaena fits in perfectly with its yellow border around light green spikes.

TIPS AND TRICKS:
- Pennisetum (also known as African feather grass) is one of several annual grasses that are popular in containers. It's drought tolerant, grows to a height of 1 metre (3 feet), and has attractive white spikes that appear later in the summer. You could substitute purple fountain grass (another variety of Pennisetum), which sends out feathery pink spikes and would look great as part of a different colour theme.
- None of these plants is a perennial, but the dracaena can be brought indoors and used as a houseplant. The rest of the plants can go in the composter once they're done for the season.

Rieger begonia (yellow)
Filler | ❀ ❀

Nemesia (yellow)
Spiller | ❀ ❀ ❀

Dracaena ('Janet Craig')
Filler | ❀

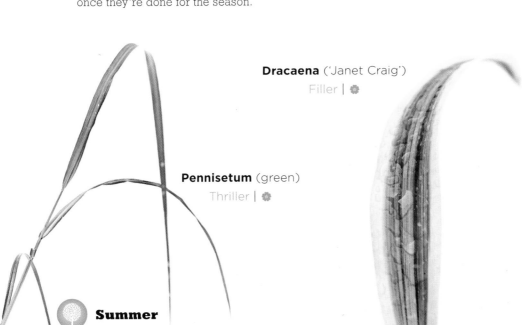

Pennisetum (green)
Thriller | ❀

Summer

259

Low
Maintenance

Bad Hair Day

SEASON: Summer

LIGHT: ☀ **WATER:** 💧💧

DESCRIPTION:
Beauty is in the eye of the beholder, and this quirky container won't suit everyone's taste. It's definitely not for the faint of heart, with its blades that shoot up like fireworks, trailing stems, twisted growth, and tongue-like features. Bad Hair Day is a collection of tropical foliage and pond plants that leans to more modern settings and looks great near a water feature. It will also do well indoors, as snake plant (also called mother-in-law's tongue) is an easy-to-care-for tropical.

TIPS AND TRICKS:
- The plants in this combo are very easy to maintain. With occasional watering and minimal fertilization, this container will survive all season long.
- Once the surrounding plants are finished, bring the snake plant indoors to enjoy for many seasons to come.

Sansevieria (snake plant)
Thriller | ✿

Dwarf umbrella palm
Thriller/Filler | ✿✿

Ornamental grass ('Fiber Optic')
Filler | ✿✿✿

Juncus (corkscrew rush)
Filler/Spiller | ✿✿

 Summer

Tropical King

SEASON: Summer

LIGHT: ☀ **WATER:** ♦♦

DESCRIPTION:

No flowers? No problem. This combo shows how just two well-matched plants can make a big impression. 'King Tut' papyrus brings this mix to regal heights: an annual grass-like plant with deep green pendulous stems and seed heads, it looks great planted close to a pond. The spill of creeping Jenny suggests the appearance of water-like movement flowing over the pot. Both creeping Jenny and papyrus lack flowers, but their interesting foliage and unique growth habits give this planter more than enough character.

TIPS AND TRICKS:

- Watering is the key to success with this container. Both creeping Jenny and 'King Tut' enjoy moist soil. I also suggest a slow-release granular fertilizer during planting to help kick-start the combo. Fertilizing later in the season is not necessary, though it helps.
- 'King Tut' grows quickly and will reach mature size by the middle of the growing season. Unfortunately, it will not overwinter.
- Creeping Jenny is a very durable perennial. I've had success overwintering it in a pot in southern Ontario, but it's safer to remove it in early fall and plant it in the garden. It's a vigorous ground cover that can take abuse even in shady locations, but if left unattended it will grow everywhere.

Cyperus
(dwarf giant papyrus 'King Tut')
Thriller | ❋

Lysimachia (creeping Jenny)
Spiller | ❋❋❋❋❋

King Kong

SEASON: Summer

LIGHT: ☀ **WATER:** 💧💧

DESCRIPTION:

Just like Tropical King (see page 263), this container packs an impact even without flowers. The name comes from the 'King Tut' grass, known for its tropical appearance and speedy growth, and the 'Kong' coleus, admired for its huge, colourful leaves that thrive in shady spaces. I've added a little Pennisetum 'Fireworks' to make this combo come alive with its colourful foliage. The pink margins of 'Fireworks' and 'Kong' link together nicely, while helping the papyrus stems to pop out. Although this combo has no spiller, the draping blades of Pennisetum and the cascading foliage of coleus have the same effect.

TIPS AND TRICKS:

- Do not put this container in direct sun or in windy spaces, or it will be torn and toppled.
- Outside of regular watering, this combo will not require deadheading and is fairly maintenance free. Occasionally you may need to remove a brown stem or two from the coleus or 'King Tut'.
- The coleus and 'King Tut' are annuals. Pennisetum 'Fireworks' is too (unless you live in Florida), but I have had success overwintering it by trimming it back in fall and leaving it to go dormant in a cold cellar—as long as the temperature does not drop below 0°C (32°F). Bring it out in spring; expose it to warmer temperatures, sunlight, regular waterings, and fertilizer; and you'll have bigger and better "fireworks" for years to come.

Coleus ('Kong')
Filler | ✿ ✿ ✿

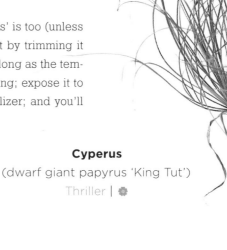

Cyperus
(dwarf giant papyrus 'King Tut')
Thriller | ✿

Pennisetum ('Fireworks')
Filler | ✿

Ferntastic

SEASON: Summer

LIGHT: ☀ **WATER:** 💧💧

DESCRIPTION:

In addition to their pleasing colour and shape, ferns help animate outdoor spaces as their foliage swings gracefully in summer breezes. The sword-shaped leaves of 'Kimberly Queen' fill as well as thrill in this lush combination. The arrowhead plant offers interest with the sharp angles and white veins of its leaves, while euphorbia 'Breathless White' spills with small white blooms, almost surrendering to the fullness of foliage above.

TIPS AND TRICKS:

- If you want a great-performing annual fern, look no farther than 'Kimberly Queen'. The easiest of all ferns to grow, it takes on its full form and great size quickly. Unlike most varieties, 'Kimberly Queen' will thrive in windy locations and in slightly sunnier areas than some other ferns, which typically require shady, sheltered spots.
- Occasional watering and biweekly fertilizing will have this container roaring to life in no time flat. In fact, I use this combo under my covered porch: it's easy, and it makes me look good—two things I like in a plant combination!

Nephthytis
(white butterfly or arrowhead plant)
Filler | ✿ ✿

Fern
('Kimberly Queen')
Thriller | ✿

Euphorbia
('Breathless White')
Spiller | ✿ ✿

Summer

Elephants and Spiders

SEASON: Summer

LIGHT: ☀ **WATER:** 💧💧

DESCRIPTION:

I like to use traditional plants in non-traditional ways. Take the spider plant, for example. It used to be one of the most common houseplants in North America, but it's rarely used outdoors. Here I've combined it with exotic elephant ears—this plant's fantastic green and pink leaves remind me of watermelon slices, and its tropical feel pairs nicely with the variegated blades of spider plant. The grey foliage of 'Silver Brocade' artemisia fills out the mix, and the red blooms of 'Caliente Hot Coral' geranium add a punch of colour.

TIPS AND TRICKS:

- The large leaves of elephant ears not only look beautiful, they also help animate this container: place the pot in a slight breeze and enjoy the plant's gentle swaying. Note that both caladium and colocasia are sometimes referred to as "Elephant Ears."
- Spider plant is easy to grow and will quickly fill out a container. If you want to bring some indoors or share it with a friend, it can be easily propagated. The stems produce baby plants with their own root systems. Just remove these and plant them in a new container with moist soil and they will quickly take root—a great activity for kids.
- Deadhead the geraniums and keep this container well watered.

Artemisia ('Silver Brocade')
Filler/Spiller | 💧💧

Spider plant
Filler/Spiller | 💧💧

Caladium (pink)
Thriller | 💧

Geranium
('Caliente Hot Coral')
Filler/Spiller | 💧💧

Summer

269

Cheerful Cherry and Yellow

SEASON: Summer

LIGHT: ☼☀   **WATER:** 💧💧

DESCRIPTION:

Love the hot, hot colours of this beautiful tropical planter? The Mandevilla is the focal point here, and its cherry pink matches perfectly with the colour of the New Guinea impatiens (commonly called sunshine impatiens). The billowing blooms of the yellow tuberous begonia pair with the similar leaf colour of the philodendron to complete the display.

TIPS AND TRICKS:

- The Mandevilla is a patio tropical, which means it can adorn your patio or deck for the summer season but must be overwintered indoors.
- At the end of the summer you can also rescue the philodendron by bringing it inside. It will make an easy-to-care-for houseplant for years to come.

Mandevilla (pink)
Thriller/Filler | ✿

Tuberous begonia (yellow)
Filler/Spiller | ✿✿✿

New Guinea impatiens (purple)
Filler | ✿

New Guinea impatiens (pink)
Filler | ✿✿

Philodendron (yellow)
Filler | ✿

Blue Velvet

SEASON: Summer

LIGHT: ☀ **WATER:** 🌢🌢

DESCRIPTION:

I love the soft, velvety blue-green leaves of the princess flower. The single purple bloom in the photo is just the promise of the blooms to come, and it matches perfectly with the 'Hot Blue' lobelia that spills from below. The red New Guinea impatiens (commonly called sunshine impatiens) offer a nice contrast to the cool blue and purple.

TIPS AND TRICKS:

- Lobelia does not like to be too hot. Keep this container in filtered light and it will perform all summer.
- We ended up with only one bloom on the princess flower on the day we shot this container, but it still looks great—just another reminder of how important it is to plant with the textures and colours of the foliage in mind as well as the blooms, so that your pots look perfect all season long.
- This combo needs to be well watered for best results.

New Guinea impatiens (red)
Filler | ✿✿✿✿

Lobelia ('Hot Blue')
Spiller | ✿✿✿

Tibouchina (princess flower blue)
Thriller | ✿

Just Peachy

SEASON: Summer

LIGHT: ☀ **WATER:** 💧💧

DESCRIPTION:

An old-fashioned porch with white wicker furniture would be the perfect setting for this planter. The showy peach blooms of the begonia and the matching peach of the impatiens fill the base of this container as the standard fuchsia rises above with its trumpet-like blooms to give the container height. The cordyline, with its pink-tipped leaves, is the finishing touch.

TIPS AND TRICKS:

- The fuchsia in this planter is a standard, which means it has been pruned to grow upright. Fuchsias are available in single, double, and clustered varieties in a wide selection of pinks and purples.
- Beware: the fuchsia will drop its blooms, and the colour can stain an unprotected surface.

Standard fuchsia
Thriller | ✿

Impatiens ('Patchwork Peach Prism')
Filler/Spiller | ✿ ✿

Cordyline
Filler | ✿

Rieger begonia (peach)
Filler | ✿ ✿

Tranquility

SEASON: Summer

LIGHT: ☼   **WATER:** 💧💧

DESCRIPTION:

The cool tones of blue, green, and purple create a tranquil setting for rest and reflection. In this mix, the soft lavender clusters of Iochroma blooms appear to nod down to the paler shades of the 'Mona Lisa' Plecanthus. Nestled between them is 'Chocolate Dark' coleus, whose leaves are so dark they are close to black. Million bells cascading down the front add yet another shade of purplish blue.

TIPS AND TRICKS:

- Using fillers with dark foliage is a great way to make bright blooms really pop out. It's like drawing on a blackboard with coloured chalk.
- I enjoy using monochromatic colour themes—it's hard to go wrong with different shades of the same colour. You can also vary the palette to change the mood. These cool shades are restful and quiet, but you could use hot colours like red and yellow to evoke happiness and energy.

Calibrachoa (million bells blue)
Spiller | 💧💧

Coleus ('Chocolate Dark')
Filler | 💧💧💧

Standard Iochroma
Thriller | 💧

Plecanthus ('Mona Lisa')
Filler | 💧💧

Summer

Mardi Gras

SEASON: Summer

LIGHT: ☀ **WATER:** 💧💧

DESCRIPTION:

If colour sets the mood of a container, this one makes me want to party. The inspiration came from the leaves of the brightly coloured croton, a fun and fantastic tropical plant. I've included both narrow and wide leaf varieties, which support the huge red 'Dragon Wing' begonias, whose vigorous growth will not only fill the pot but spill right out of it. The vibrant bicoloured blooms of the hybrid begonias and the rosettes of the million bells also pick up the shades of the croton. The hot colours of this planter are just the thing to add some Cajun heat to your landscape.

TIPS AND TRICKS:

- Place this pot in a cooler corner and keep the soil moist but not soggy. Begonias can reward you with bright rose-like blooms all summer, but the trick is in the watering. If the leaves are soft and yellowing or rotting, overwatering might be the cause. On the other hand, if the plant is parched, you'll find dry, yellowing leaves with brown tips and dropping buds.
- Begonia is prone to stem rot as well; this occurs when too much water causes the stem to soften at the base and the plant eventually collapses.

Calibrachoa (million bells yellow)
Spiller | ✿ ✿

Wide leaf croton
Filler | ✿ ✿

Begonia ('Dragon Wing' red)
Thriller/Filler/Spiller | ✿ ✿

Rieger begonia
(yellow and orange)
Filler | ✿ ✿ ✿

Narrow leaf croton
Filler | ✿

Summer

In the Pink

Nephthytis
(white butterfly or arrowhead plant)
Filler | ✿

SEASON: Summer

LIGHT: ☼   **WATER:** ♦♦

DESCRIPTION:
I love the simple elegance of these calla lilies, with their purple trumpets and a trace of pink rising above the dark spotted foliage. This pink is repeated in the luminous shade of the begonia, surrounded by the tiny white torenia (also known as wishbone flower) that spill over the side of the pot. The pale green leaves of the arrowhead plant form a sharp contrast to the black leaves of the coleus nestled within.

Coleus (black)
Filler | ✿✿

TIPS AND TRICKS:
- Callas grow from a rhizome that must be planted in spring to bloom in summer. The rhizomes won't overwinter in colder climates, but you can remove them after the first hard frost, storing them in a cool, dark, dry place, to reuse year after year.
- Although you can purchase the rhizomes in late winter and start them yourself indoors in March or April, they are sold as potted plants in spring at garden centres.

Double tuberous begonia (pink)
Filler | ✿✿

Double impatiens (white)
Filler | ✿✿

Torenia (white)
Filler/Spiller | ✿✿

Calla (lily black)
Thriller | ✿

Summer

Aloha!

SEASON: Summer

LIGHT: ☀ **WATER:** 💧💧

DESCRIPTION:

Capture the beauty of Hawaii in a pot. The 'Fiber Optic' ornamental grass on the side of this container mimics the grass skirt of a hula dancer, while exotic-looking impatiens sit under a millet "palm tree." Backing all of this is the dark foliage of coleus, with its delicate pink vein. The perfect combo to enjoy with a Blue Hawaii!

TIPS AND TRICKS:

- The 'Jester' variety of millet grass is one of several that have come on the market specifically for containers. It starts the season in lime with a burgundy vein, then gradually changes to burgundy, and then to bronze.
- The compact 'Fiber Optic' grass gets its name from the tiny flowers at the tips of the blades. It's great for containers both indoors and out, and even performs well in water gardens.
- Although the grasses here are meant for full sun, they will also do well in part sun, as long as they get a few hours of direct rays each day.

Millet ('Jester')
Thriller | ☀

Ornamental grass
('Fiber Optic')
Spiller | ☀☀

Impatiens ('Patchwork Peach Prism')
Filler/Spiller | ☀☀

Dark leaf coleus
Thriller/Filler | ☀☀

Summer

Soft Sunrise

SEASON: Summer

LIGHT: ☀ **WATER:** 💧💧

DESCRIPTION:

The feathery foliage of button fern settles like morning dew along the base of this planter; lobelia and coleus rise up beside the corkscrew rush, which has the appearance of chives. The cherry blooms of the geraniums complete this mix, which has the feel of a sunrise on a quiet summer morning. Whenever I look at it, it inspires hope in me for the day ahead.

TIPS AND TRICKS:

- Ferns come in an array of leaf types, sizes, and colours, and although they are often used as fillers, some have a flowing habit that allows them to play the role of spiller. Spillers do not need to trail—they just need to flow beyond the pot's lip.
- Button ferns, coleus, geraniums, and corkscrew rush are not frost tolerant, but the lobelia can be salvaged and planted in the garden.
- Deadhead the geraniums all season to keep them blooming.

Fern

Filler/Spiller | ✿ ✿

Perennial lobelia
('Queen Victoria')

Thriller | ✿ ✿

Coleus ('Versa Rose to Lime')

Filler | ✿

Geranium (red)

Filler | ✿ ✿

Juncus
(corkscrew rush)

Thriller | ✿

Summer

287

Sparkling White

SEASON: Summer

LIGHT: ☀ **WATER:** 💧💧

DESCRIPTION:

The gardenia in this combo thrills both the eyes and the nose: its radiant white double flowers have a sultry fragrance. This one is pruned to standard form so its dark green glossy foliage towers over the other plants. White torenia and nicotiana (also called tobacco plant) blooms fill the bottom of the container and complement the gardenia; the grey foliage of dusty miller and the silver stripes of peperomia add a bit of character.

TIPS AND TRICKS:

- Gardenias are sold mostly as a flowering houseplant and enjoyed for their beauty and scent. You can grow them outdoors in summer, but keep them out of direct sun and wind. Gardenias also love humidity, so it's a good idea to mist them regularly to prevent bud drop. Don't get water on the blooms themselves, however, or they will discolour.
- Dusty miller is an underrated foliage plant that can add so much to any container. When it's paired with pink or white, its grey leaves make other colours pop.
- The heart-shaped, striped leaves of peperomia add an extra layer of interest to this pot. This is also a common houseplant that you can bring indoors at the end of the season.

Nicotiana (white)
Filler | ❀❀❀❀❀❀

Standard gardenia (white)
Thriller | ❀

Peperomia ('Watermelon')
Filler | ❀❀

Torenia (white)
Spiller | ❀❀❀

Dusty miller ('Silver Dust')
Filler | ❀❀❀

Summer

Deep Purple

SEASON: Summer

LIGHT: ☀   **WATER:** ♦♦

DESCRIPTION:

This planter is a stunning combination of purples and blues. It draws your eyes immediately with the silvery foliage of the Russian sage rising up behind the spires of blue salvia. 'Midnight Blue' petunias deliver a punch with their huge, bold blooms. Trailing lobelia adds the finishing touch.

TIPS AND TRICKS:

• Russian sage is a great perennial in the late-summer garden, its tall, wispy stems filling up with tiny lavender or blue flowers. Its appearance and colour make it a pretty companion with roses or black-eyed Susan. It will be fine in part shade, but it performs best in full sun.

• You can transplant the Russian sage in your garden, but the other plants are one-year wonders.

Russian sage (blue)
Thriller | ❁❁❁

Salvia ('Mystic Spires Blue')
Thriller | ❁❁❁

Lobelia ('Hot Blue')
Spiller | ❁❁❁❁

Petunia ('Midnight Blue')
Filler | ❁❁❁❁

 **Summer**

Taro Lime

SEASON: Summer

LIGHT: ☼●   **WATER:** 💧💧

DESCRIPTION:
'Imperial Taro' steals the show in this combo and immediately invokes a feeling of the tropics. The colour story here is a mixture of foliage complemented by pink and violet flowers. This hot-looking container will thrive in a shady space, as tuberous begonia, impatiens, and creeping Jenny all enjoy low light. Even if the impatiens or begonias underperform, this combination will still look great thanks to the contrasting foliage colours, leaf sizes, and textures.

TIPS AND TRICKS:
- Two things this mixture will not tolerate are direct sun and wind. The plants are not drought tolerant and will need regular watering to keep them looking good. In a windy location, 'Imperial Taro' will be torn to ribbons and the foliage of the begonias and impatiens will dry out.
- Creeping Jenny is a perennial, so after enjoying it in the container, you can plant it in the garden in fall. But be warned: creeping Jenny does creep. It can send runners into your lawn and can easily become a weed if left uncared for.
- The bulbs of 'Imperial Taro' can be harvested in fall and stored indoors in a cool, dark, dry place for planting next spring.

Tuberous begonia
('Nonstop Mocca Pink')
Filler | ✿✿

Colocasia ('Imperial Taro')
Thriller | ✿✿

Lysimachia (creeping Jenny)
Spiller | ✿✿✿✿

Impatiens ('Dazzler' violet)
Filler | ✿✿

Marshland

SEASON: Summer

LIGHT: ☼●   **WATER:** 💧💧

DESCRIPTION:

I was lucky enough to grow up in the country, and I often went on adventures in search of tadpoles, dragonflies, and minnows. This container reminds me of those days. It includes a variety of foliage that combines to create a natural feel. The whimsical arching of dwarf giant papyrus reminds me of bulrushes, while the trailing habit of pothos (a philodendron) and German ivy recalls water lilies and water lettuce in marshland areas. Although this combo may lack colour, it's rich with interest and will have a cool, calming effect in any environment.

TIPS AND TRICKS:

- What inspires you? For this combination, the discovery of a dragonfly pick brought back childhood memories and inspired me to search out plants that resembled the marshland where I grew up. When creating a container, find something to inspire a theme and allow that to guide your plant selections.
- This is an almost care-free container. All you need to do is monitor it for water and fertilize once or twice.
- This combination includes some common houseplants—pothos, spider plant, and German ivy—so it can be enjoyed both indoors and out.

German ivy
Spiller | ✿✿

Pothos (variegated)
Spiller | ✿✿

Spider plant
Spiller | ✿✿✿

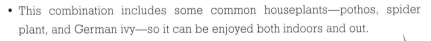

Cyperus
(dwarf giant papyrus 'Gracilis')
Filler | ✿

Strawberry Dazzler

SEASON: Summer

LIGHT: ☀●   **WATER:** 💧💧

DESCRIPTION:

Rex begonia (sometimes known as strawberry begonia) is the central character in this container story. Its uniquely shaped leaves remind me of stained-glass windows, with their interesting mosaic of pink, purple, grey, and white. The deep green veins of variegated English ivy and the boldness of 'Dazzler' pink impatiens create an enjoyable combination of shade-loving plants that will help brighten up the darker spaces on your property.

TIPS AND TRICKS:

- Found a plant with cool foliage but have no idea what to match it with? Don't be afraid to remove a leaf and hold it up to other plants to see if they look good together. I do this often—in fact, at the garden centre I will set up a number of plants alongside each other to see how they look together. Sometimes the garden centre owners don't like it, but if they are savvy, they know what I'm doing and that they're about to make a sale.
- Never place this combination in direct afternoon sun. Like people, shade-loving plants can get sunburned. The soft, water-filled leaves of rex begonia and impatiens are especially prone to sun scorch.

Impatiens ('Dazzler' pink)
Filler | ✿✿✿✿

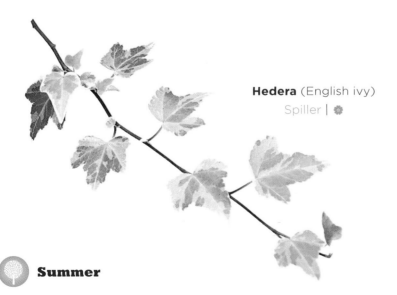

Hedera (English ivy)
Spiller | ✿

Rex begonia
Thriller | ✿

Made in the Shade

SEASON: Summer

LIGHT: ☀◐●   **WATER:** ♦♦♦

DESCRIPTION:

Here's a great-performing planter that is made in the shade. The white double rosette flowers of the impatiens create a sharp contrast with the brooding foliage of coleus 'Chocolate Mint', making this container shine in low light. The blue trumpet-shaped blooms of torenia are also effective alongside the white impatiens: the two colours evoke memories of snow and cool water and spell relief on a hot summer day.

TIPS AND TRICKS:

- Torenia (also known as wishbone flower) is an underused plant. It's a vigorous grower with a long bloom period and a trailing habit that makes it an ideal spiller in a shade-loving container.
- The plants in this combination despise being dried out. The trick is to give them enough water to keep them moist, but not too much, as impatiens and torenia can rot. Morning waterings are always best.

Torenia (blue)
Spiller | ✿✿

Double impatiens (white)
Thriller/Filler | ✿✿✿✿

Coleus ('Chocolate Mint')
Thriller/Filler | ✿

Bonfire

SEASON: Summer

LIGHT: ☀◐●   **WATER:** 💧💧

DESCRIPTION:

With dramatic foliage and bold orange blooms, this combination suggests the warmth of a summer bonfire and is a proven performer in the shade. I absolutely love 'Angel Wing' begonias—I find their flowers dramatic, and their foliage gives any container continuous interest. They also partner well in form and colour with 'Dazzler' orange impatiens, and both are echoed in the colourful foliage of coleus 'Versa Watermelon'.

TIPS AND TRICKS:

- In some spaces, you may not want a container with great height. The plants in this combo like to lay low, but their bright, bold colours jump out at you and create a huge impact. When deciding on a colour scheme, think about the mood you want to create. Orange brings excitement, and when used in large, shady spaces, it will liven up even the darkest settings.
- This container needs minimal care: just water when the soil is dry.

Impatiens ('Dazzler' orange)
Filler | ❀❀❀❀❀❀

Coleus ('Versa Watermelon')
Thriller | ❀❀❀

Begonia ('Angel Wing')
Filler | ❀❀❀

A Pot of Substance

SEASON: Summer

LIGHT: ☀●   **WATER:** ♦♦

DESCRIPTION:
'Sum and Substance' is one of my favourite hostas. I love its big, bright leaves and the pure white blooms that sit atop its long spikes. The soft foliage of maidenhair fern, the deep green leaves and bright lilac blooms of the New Guinea (or sunshine) impatiens, the spill of wine periwinkle, and the bright blades of Hakone grass all come together to complement the hosta in this shade-loving container. The foliage plants here offer a lot of variety in leaf size, colour, and texture, which adds interest even when the flowering plants are not in bloom.

TIPS AND TRICKS:
- Don't let this container get sunburned. If you place it in the afternoon sunshine, you'll burn the leaves of the hosta and fry the grass.
- Removing dead or decaying foliage, regular watering, and occasional fertilizing will keep this combo in tip-top shape throughout the season. After the hosta flowers have finished, cut the flower spikes at the base.
- I've had success overwintering both periwinkle and 'Sum and Substance' hosta in a pot, but it really depends on the severity of the winter. To be safe, you may just want to plant these perennials in the ground in the fall. The maidenhair fern can go in the garden too.

Wine periwinkle
Spiller | ✿

New Guinea impatiens
('Super Sonic Lilac')
Filler | ✿

American maidenhair fern
Filler/Spiller | ✿ ✿

Hakone grass
('All Gold')
Filler | ✿

Hosta ('Sum and Substance')
Thriller | ✿

 Summer

Tropical Breezes

SEASON: Summer

LIGHT: ☀●   **WATER:** 💧💧

DESCRIPTION:

Perfect for a spot with filtered light, this planter recalls memories of tropical holidays—it almost makes me want a daiquiri! The yellow-edged leaves of the 'Lemon Lime' dracaena contrast beautifully with the dark foliage of the false aralia behind it. The wide leaves of the maidenhair fern give the combo a lush look as it intermingles with the button fern. The staghorn fern adds interest as it juts over the side of the container.

TIPS AND TRICKS:

- You might think this planter could handle full sun, but these tropical plants naturally live on the jungle floor under huge leafy canopies. You can mimic that environment by placing this container in the dappled light of a large tree on your property.
- This planter is very low maintenance. There is no deadheading and no dropped petals. Just keep it watered and fertilized throughout the summer and you could bring it to the office for the winter.

Dracaena
('Lemon Lime')
Filler | ✿

American maidenhair fern
Filler | ✿

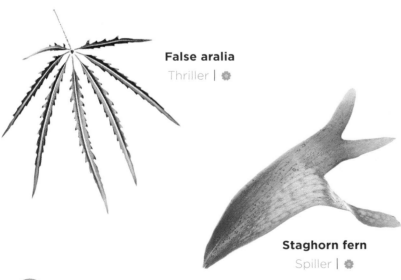

False aralia
Thriller | ✿

Staghorn fern
Spiller | ✿

Button fern
Spiller | ✿

Summer

Peace and Quiet

Loves Shady Spaces

SEASON: Summer

LIGHT: ☀●   **WATER:** ♦♦♦

DESCRIPTION:
The claim to fame of the peace lily are its lush, shiny, deep green leaves and its showy white bowl-shaped flowers. A tropical that thrives in low light, peace lilies are popular houseplants that help purify indoor air. In this container, we've combined it with torenia, which produces non-stop blue trumpet-shaped flowers in some of the shadiest spaces. This simple mix creates a big impact but still gives a peaceful impression.

TIPS AND TRICKS:
- Peace lilies are extremely sensitive to light. Yellow tips or brown patches on leaves may indicate that it's getting too much sun.
- The challenge with torenia is that it's susceptible to powdery mildew. Make sure this container gets good air circulation, and give it an occasional spray with a fungicide.

Spathiphyllum (peace lily white)
Thriller | ✿

Torenia (blue)
Spiller | ✿✿✿

Summer

ZZ Top

SEASON: Summer

LIGHT: ☀●   **WATER:** 💧💧

DESCRIPTION:

The funky ZZ plant doesn't get its name from the Texas rock band with the crazy beards. The moniker comes from its scientific name: *Zamioculcas zamiifolia*. It adds thrill to this container with its tropical palm-like stems, which are complemented by the foliage of rex begonia and the dainty feathery stems of the fern. The colour burst in this combo comes from the dwarf fuchsia blooms at the bottom.

TIPS AND TRICKS:

- ZZ plant is the ultimate choice for brown thumbs. It will survive in a wide range of conditions, from no light to bright light, from lots of water to no water. However, for best results, keep your ZZ in part sun and water it only when it's completely dry. At the end of the growing season, bring it inside and enjoy it as a houseplant.
- Fuchsia adds brilliant colour to a container and will attract hummingbirds. But don't place this pot on your expensive patio: the flowers will fall and they can stain stone and concrete.

ZZ plant
Thriller | ✿

Dwarf fuchsia
Spiller | ✿ ✿ ✿

Rex begonia
Filler | ✿

Fern
Filler | ✿

Summer

Fairy Candle

SEASON: Summer

LIGHT: ☀ **WATER:** 💧💧

DESCRIPTION:

Fairy candle is a common name for black snakeroot, a perennial woodland plant with dark leaves and spiky flowers that bloom in the deepest shade and resemble a tall candle flame. (It's past its bloom in this photo.) Black snakeroot (also called black cohosh) has long been used in herbal remedies, and even today it is often used to treat menopause symptoms. Here it provides the backdrop for a mat of pale pink impatiens and a jungle of periwinkle.

TIPS AND TRICKS:

- Periwinkle is a great perennial to use as a spiller. It's hardy and drought tolerant and does well in any condition, from full sun to full shade. It can grow to a length of 120 cm (4 feet) or longer and looks fantastic in raised urns or high window boxes.
- Impatiens really don't do well if they're allowed to dry out. As soon as you start to see the leaves curl up, you're losing them, so keep them well watered.

Impatiens (pink)
Filler | ❀ ❀ ❀

Periwinkle (variegated)
Spiller | ❀ ❀

Black snakeroot
Thriller | ❀

Watch Your Tongue

SEASON: Summer/Fall

LIGHT: ○ ◐ ◑ ●   **WATER:** ▲

DESCRIPTION:

Sansevieria—this variety is called mother-in-law's tongue or snake plant—has so much to offer that it doesn't need any help in this container. This tropical plant has stiff, upright leaves with a variegated pattern and sharp tips. The simplicity of this planter, with its bold straight lines, makes it the perfect accessory on your deck or balcony.

TIPS AND TRICKS:

- Sansevieria is nearly indestructible. It's so versatile that you can use it outdoors much of the year and bring it inside as a houseplant in winter. If you use it outside, keep in mind that it prefers part sun, though it will adjust to full sun. Indoors, it can withstand dry air, drafts, and your holidays away from home. This plant will not withstand temperatures below freezing, overwatering, or not watering at all—otherwise you are assured success.

Sansevieria (snake plant)

Shady Character

SEASON: Summer

LIGHT: ☀   **WATER:** 💧💧

DESCRIPTION:
This planter is perfect for bringing nature into a darker corner of your property, thanks to a combination of shade-loving plants and bright blooms. The ostrich fern adds height and movement, while the glossy foliage of the Japanese spurge paired with the dark green foliage of impatiens provide the backdrop for the crisp white flowers.

TIPS AND TRICKS:
- At the end of the season, the two perennials in this mix can be overwintered in the container in a protected area, or transplanted in the garden for years of enjoyment.
- Ostrich ferns can grow to a height of 1 metre (3 feet) or more and will thrive in the shade as long as you keep the soil moist. If the soil dries out, the fern will become brown and wither quickly. Plant this fern in a moist, shady corner of the garden and it will multiply by sending out lateral stolons to produce new plants. Grouped under tall trees, ostrich ferns give a cool, restful look to the garden.
- Japanese spurge is a great ground cover for shade, with shiny green leaves that always look fresh. It is also available with a variegated leaf, white and green, that is not as aggressive a grower. This plant is great to grow in the deeply shaded parts of your property where nothing else grows.

Ostrich fern
Thriller | ❀

Impatiens (white)
Filler/Spiller | ❀ ❀ ❀

Japanese spurge
Filler | ❀ ❀

Summer

Pleasantly Pink

SEASON: Summer

LIGHT: **WATER:** ●●

DESCRIPTION:

Flowers and foliage in every shape and size are united in this combo by the colour pink. The feathery display of astilbe, the rose-like bloom of begonia, and the tiny flowers of the lungwort all share the same raspberry shade—even the leaf of the bugleweed has a hint of pink. (It blooms with a bright blue flower in spring.) This pretty planter will flourish in the dappled shade of a mature yard.

TIPS AND TRICKS:

- Bugleweed is a great ground cover for shade and is available in a variety of colours, from green to green-white to dark burgundy. Bugleweed requires frequent watering to get started, but once it's established it spreads by runners and can get invasive. It's ideal for filling up a large area quickly, but if you transplant it from the pot, place it where its growth can be contained in some way—for example, use edging if you plant it near your lawn.
- Astilbe and lungwort are also shade-loving perennials. Astilbe is available in shades of red, pink, purple, and white and in different heights. Plant it in an area of your yard that won't dry out, as this plant likes to have wet feet. Neither plant does well in the heat, so choose an area of the garden under a big tree, with a hose close at hand.

Pulmonaria
(lungwort 'Raspberry Splash')
Filler |

Ajuga
(bugleweed 'Burgundy Glow')
Spiller |

Tuberous begonia
('Nonstop Mocca Pink')
Filler | ● ●

Astilbe ('Montgomery')
Thriller |

Undercover

SEASON: Summer

LIGHT: ☀ **WATER:** 💧💧

DESCRIPTION:

When you hear the word "chameleon," you probably think of something you won't notice because it blends in with its surroundings. That definitely does not describe the amazing chameleon plant. It gets its name because its normally green and white foliage changes to brilliant shades of pink, orange, and red during the growing season. At different times, it will complement the spring green of foxtail fern and the bright orange of the impatiens. The bronze foliage of the rex begonia also has an orange underside that's as colourful as the impatiens, making this a container with lots of hidden surprises.

TIPS AND TRICKS:

- People either love or hate the chameleon plant. On the positive side, it not only adds a lot of interest in a container but is also is a perennial ground cover that spreads easily in any type of soil (it prefers moisture) and in sun or shade. On the negative side, it's a perennial ground cover that spreads easily. Chameleon plant is invasive in the garden and very difficult to get rid of. You're probably best to grow it only in a container.
- The chameleon plant has a very strong lemony scent. This is helpful in deterring rabbits from your garden—but it also deters a lot of people!
- Foxtail fern (also called asparagus fern) likes to have wet feet, so keep it well watered.

Impatiens (orange)
Thriller | ❁

Foxtail fern
Thriller | ❁

Rex begonia
Filler | ❁

Houttunia (chameleon plant)
Filler | ❁

Frosted Sunrise

SEASON: Summer

LIGHT: ☼◕   **WATER:** 💧💧

DESCRIPTION:

Want to capture the beauty of dawn all day long? Look no farther than this stunning planter. The frosty foliage of brunnera 'Looking Glass' creates a wonderful backdrop for the blooms of 'Nonstop Mocca Deep Orange' tuberous begonias, which make me think of the rising sun. The arching blades of 'Silver Dragon' lilyturf create a spill, while the jagged leaves of 'Sugar and Spice' foam flower fill out the setting. Together these plants offer a unique combination that will perform well in a shady spot.

TIPS AND TRICKS:

- Here's another example of why your container's thriller doesn't need to have dramatic height: the fantastic leaves of brunnera 'Looking Glass' really draw the eye. I selected the other plants to contrast with the foliage or complement its colour.
- Brunnera, lilyturf, and foam flower are all perennials that can be removed and replanted in the garden in late fall. However, if you want to take a stab at overwintering them in the container, plant the whole pot in the ground—the surrounding soil will help insulate the roots. If you don't have room in the garden, try placing the container in a cold cellar or unheated garage, where it will undergo its dormant period without getting too frosty.

Brunnera ('Looking Glass')
Thriller | ✿✿

Tuberous begonia
('Nonstop Mocca Deep Orange')
Filler | ✿✿✿

Lilyturf ('Silver Dragon')
Spiller | ✿✿

Foam flower ('Sugar and Spice')
Filler | ✿

 **Summer**

Soft Shade

SEASON: Summer

LIGHT: ☀●   **WATER:** ♦♦♦

DESCRIPTION:

Three fabulous shade-loving varieties of hosta are the foundation of this planter. The blue of 'Elegans' contrasts with the yellow, white, and green of 'Fire and Ice' and 'Whirling Dervish', and the difference in leaf size and character adds another dimension of interest. The variegated 'Stairway to Heaven' Jacob's ladder complements the hosta, while the pure white blooms of sweet woodruff cascade over the pot.

TIPS AND TRICKS:

- What's not to love about hostas? They offer endless options when it comes to leaf size, colour, variegation, and shape, and they're reliable performers in the shade. Over the years, I've even had good success overwintering most varieties in a container.
- Jacob's ladder and sweet woodruff are excellent potted partners, but plant them in the garden after enjoying them in the container.
- Fertilizing once a month is plenty for this tough combo.

Hosta ('Fire and Ice')
Thriller/Filler | ✿

Hosta ('Elegans')
Thriller/Filler | ✿

Jacob's ladder
('Stairway to Heaven')
Filler | ✿

Sweet woodruff
Spiller | ✿✿

Hosta ('Whirling Dervish')
Thriller/Filler | ✿

 **Summer**

Croton

SEASON: Summer/Fall

LIGHT: ☼ ☼   **WATER:** ♦♦

DESCRIPTION:

Why not bring a little of the tropics to your backyard? Just one look at this vivid foliage and I'm reminded of holidays in Florida and Mexico. Croton is a fantastic woody plant with big, waxy, colourfully veined leaves that has long been a popular houseplant. I think it also looks great on the deck in summer.

TIPS AND TRICKS:

- The foliage colour of croton depends on the light it receives. If the plant is left in hot, direct sun—or if it doesn't get enough light—the leaves will lose some of their vivid shades. To keep it looking its best, water your croton often, not letting it dry out, and fertilize it throughout the summer.
- Monitor your plant for the webbing of red spider mites and scale (tiny hard-shelled insects). Spray with insecticidal soap if you notice any lurking pests.
- In fall, before the temperature drops to freezing, bring your croton indoors. Place it in an east- or west-facing window, in a warm room with no drafts. Water less often and do not fertilize. In spring, once the risk of frost has passed, harden off the plant by giving it a few hours of full sun each day for a week or two, bringing it indoors at night.
- Croton is toxic, so keep it away from children who might be attracted by its colourful appearance.

Croton
Thriller | ✿

Summer

Fall

Cooler nights, enjoying the harvest of fruits and vegetables, and nature's final explosion of colour—this is why fall is my favourite season. The autumn container garden should celebrate the colours of the season: oranges, reds, burgundy, and purple. The threat of frost has returned, but that means you get to enjoy fantastic plants like flowering cabbage and kale, ornamental grasses, mums, and other legends of the fall.

Dark Night

SEASON: Late summer/Fall

LIGHT: ☼☼   **WATER:** ⬤⬤

DESCRIPTION:
The longer, cooler nights of autumn inspired the rich, velvety colours of this container. The underplantings invoke a nighttime feel, with black violas and dark purple flowering cabbage, brightened by a light purple garden mum, with its daisy-like flowers. The green fountain grass offers contrasting foliage and an eruption of green. This frost-hardy combination adds drama to an autumn evening on the patio.

TIPS AND TRICKS:
- Place this container in an open area so you can enjoy the animation of the ornamental grass during breezy fall days.
- Fall mums are technically perennials, but many do not overwinter. The other plants in this mix are annuals, so this whole container can go in the compost pile at the end of the season.
- To create a Halloween look for this container, add small ornamental pumpkins and cotton cobwebs.
- This combo needs only very occasional watering.

Flowering cabbage (purple)
Filler/Spiller | ✿✿✿

Chrysanthemum (purple)
Filler | ✿

Green fountain grass
Thriller | ✿

Viola (black)
Filler/Spiller | ✿✿✿✿✿

Harvest Dawn

SEASON: Fall

LIGHT: ☼◑   **WATER:** 💧💧

DESCRIPTION:

As mornings start to get crisp and the leaves begin to turn, my thoughts turn to apple pies in my belly and lush combinations of orange and red in my containers. This mix of garden mums, pansies, coneflower, and millet sets the tone for the fall. With its corn-like appearance, millet creates a feeling of the harvest; the underplantings of chrysanthemums and pansies pack a punch; and a single coneflower adds additional interest.

TIPS AND TRICKS:

- Purple millet is an awesome choice for fall. With fantastic foliage and bird-attracting seed heads, this plant adds height, impact, and colour to any container. However, frost is its downfall. For those of you who live in an area where it drops below freezing in early fall, I suggest you lean away from purple millet. Dried corn stalks are a good substitute.
- Pansies and mums can handle below-freezing temperatures; coneflower is a perennial that will easily overwinter in the garden.
- Water this combo regularly, but don't fertilize after September 1.

Pansy (red)
Spiller | ✿✿✿

Pansy (orange)
Spiller | ✿✿✿

Chrysanthemum (orange)
Filler | ✿

Chrysanthemum (red)
Filler | ✿

Echinacea
(coneflower 'Fatal Attraction')
Filler | ✿

Millet (purple)
Thriller | ✿

 Fall

Old Holly Hubbard

SEASON: Late summer/Fall

LIGHT: ○◐   **WATER:** 💧💧

DESCRIPTION:

With its hint of winter, this combination reminds us that the end of the growing season is near. 'Berri-Magic China' holly, with its glossy, spiky foliage and red berries, even teases us with thoughts of Christmas. Plantings of red blanket flower and pansies alongside the thrill of red fountain grass create a complementary mix of flowers and foliage that ties in with the red holly berries. Finally, I've accessorized with a Hubbard squash to pay tribute to the harvest and make this an ideal container for your Thanksgiving entrance display.

TIPS AND TRICKS:

- When creating a fall feel, you can look to the colours of the forest, or you can look in the produce aisle. If you're going to use natural accessories in a pot, choose ones that can handle the outdoor environment in fall. With warm days and cool nights, the tough skin of Hubbard squash will hold up well.
- Unlike most other varieties of holly, 'Berri-Magic China' has a compact form that makes it ideal for pots. It's also unusual in being a self-pollinator. (Most other varieties of holly have both male and female plants; only the female plants bear fruit, but you need a male nearby to provide pollen.) You can plant the holly in the garden just before snow flies.
- Water regularly and eliminate all fertilizing by early fall.

Holly ('Berri-Magic China')
Filler | ✿

Pansy (red)
Spiller | ✿ ✿ ✿

Gaillardia (blanket flower red)
Filler | ✿ ✿

Red fountain grass
Thriller | ✿

 Fall

337

Cool as Kale

SEASON: Late summer/Fall/Early winter

LIGHT: ☼☼   **WATER:** 💧💧

DESCRIPTION:
A new fall classic. With just three types of plants, this container is as easy as it is cool. With mounding form and contrasting foliage of blue, purple, green, and burgundy, the flowering cabbage and kale fill and spill, while the graceful blades of green fountain grass supply the thrill with their height and graceful movement. This pot will add interest to your property from late summer right up until the first breath of winter.

TIPS AND TRICKS:
- In addition to its vibrant colours, this container is a tough late-season performer: the cabbage and kale can handle cold nights and warm days. The colours will become even richer as the temperature falls.
- Water this pot only when it dries out and do not fertilize. Inspect the leaves of the cabbage and kale for holes. If you see any, spray with insecticidal soap.

Green fountain grass
Thriller | ✿✿

Flowering cabbage (white)
Filler/Spiller | ✿✿✿

Flowering kale (purple)
Filler/Spiller | ✿✿✿

 Fall

Season's Change

SEASON: Fall

LIGHT: ☼☼   **WATER:** ♦♦♦

DESCRIPTION:

As summer gives way to fall, plants reveal their true colours. This container, a combination of annuals and shrubs, celebrates fantastic fall foliage and creates an eye-catching display without a single flower. The vibrant reds of dwarf American cranberry contrast against the lime-green foliage of 'Endless Summer' hydrangea and the burgundy blades of red fountain grass, while the frilled leaves of red flowering kale spill over the side.

TIPS AND TRICKS:

- Although both dwarf American cranberry and 'Endless Summer' hydrangea bloom during the summer, fall foliage is their real strength. Plant both of them in the garden after enjoying them in the container.
- Cranberry is actually a three-season hero, offering white blooms in late spring, red foliage in fall, and red berries in late fall and winter. You could plant cranberry in a container in early spring and surround it with pansies, and then give it a summer makeover by replacing the pansies with petunias. In the fall, take out the petunias and plant this combo.
- Flowering kale can tolerate extremely chilly temperatures. In fact, the intensity of its colour increases as it gets colder. However, this is truly an annual plant. The best way kale and fountain grass can contribute to future gardens is by being added to the compost pile.
- With reduced daylight and more rain in fall, this container requires only occasional watering and no fertilization.

Dwarf American cranberry
Thriller | ✿

Flowering kale (dark red)
Spiller | ✿

Red fountain grass
Filler/Spiller | ✿

Hydrangea ('Endless Summer')
Filler | ✿

 Fall

341

Hardy Canadian

Weeping Canadian hemlock
Thriller | ❁

SEASON: Fall/Early winter

LIGHT: ☼◐ **WATER:** 💧💧

DESCRIPTION:

Good old Jack Frost usually spells the end of summer plantings, but he also encourages you to go for a new look. This combination of evergreen, perennial, and annual plants is ideal for late-summer planting: you'll have a unique container that will thrive through fall and early winter. The drooping evergreen stems of weeping Canadian hemlock create the thrill, and the underplantings of sage, asters, dusty miller, and flowering cabbage asters add brilliant colour and interesting foliage. This creative container is perfect for nature lovers and those of you who like to showcase native Canadian plants.

Flowering cabbage (purple)
Spiller | ❁

TIPS AND TRICKS:

• When creating containers for fall and winter, keep the cooler temperatures in mind. Here I've combined late summer– and fall-blooming perennials alongside frost-tolerant plants with fantastic foliage. This allows you to enjoy great colour during warmer days and keeps your container interesting even when the nights dip below freezing.

• Evergreen thrillers like hemlock can easily get a seasonal update. For example, Winter Reflections on page 373 shows you how to give this pot a Christmas look.

• Remove the spent flowers and cut back the asters after blooming.

• Water regularly on warm, sunny days, but back off during cooler temperatures and on cloudy days. This plant doesn't need any fertilizing; with late-season plants like hemlock, you want to slow down new growth as you harden them off for winter.

• The hemlock will not usually overwinter in the container, but you can plant it in the garden.

Aster ('Magic')
Filler | ❁

Dusty miller
Filler/Spiller | ❁ ❁ ❁

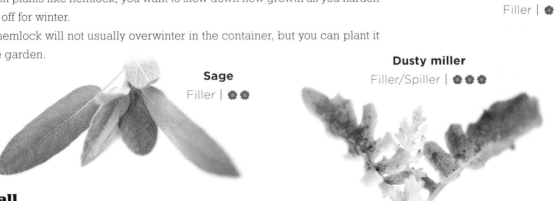

Sage
Filler | ❁ ❁

Winter

Snowflakes, icicles, the crackle of a fire, the cosy feel of a down-filled duvet—time to snuggle up for the winter. You can continue making beautiful containers long after freeze-up, but now your job is more like a florist's than a gardener's. Outdoor containers must be built to survive the weather with a combination of evergreen boughs, interesting stems, and brightly coloured accessories. They're the ideal way to keep your home looking cheerful during the holidays.

Jolly Jester

SEASON: Christmas

LIGHT: ☼◐◑●   **WATER:** 💧

DESCRIPTION:

Fun, playful, glamorous—what's not to love about this dramatic Christmas display? The solid base of traditional evergreen boughs is accessorized with a collection of gold balls, spray picks, and gold leaf picks, all topped with a huge gold cone. This holiday combo will have your neighbours talking and your children smiling right into the New Year.

TIPS AND TRICKS:

- The challenge with this container is keeping the evergreens from drying out during periods of frost-free weather in early winter. I recommend placing the picks in floral foam soaked in water rather than using potting soil. The floral foam not only allows for better form (it will hold the stems up) but will also retain moisture to feed the boughs when required.

Evergreen boughs
(fir, pine, cedar, spruce)
Filler

Accessories

Cone (gold) | 💧
Decorative ball (gold) | 💧💧💧
Spray pick (gold) | 💧💧💧
Leaf pick (gold) | 💧💧💧💧

Winter

Apple Twist

SEASON: Winter/Christmas

LIGHT: ☼◐◑● **WATER:** 💧

DESCRIPTION:

Inside every adult is a child with visions of candy apples and toys on Christmas Day. This whimsical, magical combination evokes the excitement of the holidays. A spiral grapevine tree rises up from a bed of evergreens, accented with dogwood stems and real apples used as ornaments. A few picks of red artificial berries contrast nicely with the fresh stems of pine, fir, cedar, and spruce.

With two children under age four, I read a lot of kids' books, and Dr. Seuss is one of my favourites. I wanted to create a container that shouted out fun, while at the same time staying as natural as possible. By itself, the spiral twig tree added height, but it lacked the charm I was looking for. So I decided to add some red apples secured with wire, as well as red dogwood stems, to up the fun factor.

TIPS AND TRICKS:

- Don't use real apples in this planter if you have deer or raccoons in your area. Invest in plastic ones instead.
- Water this container occasionally to keep the boughs fresh until freeze-up.

Evergreen boughs
(fir, pine, cedar, spruce)
Filler

Accessories

Apple (red) | 💧💧💧💧💧💧💧💧💧💧💧💧
Berry pick | 💧💧💧
Spiral grapevine tree | 💧

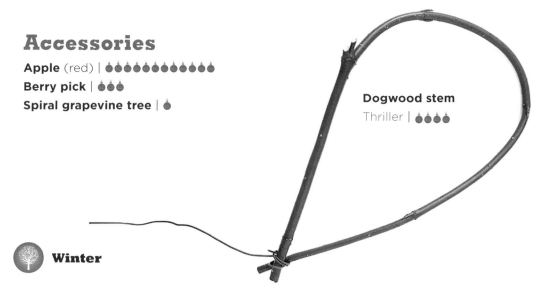

Dogwood stem
Thriller | 💧💧💧💧

Winter Wings

SEASON: Winter/Christmas

LIGHT: ○◑◐● **WATER:** ◔

DESCRIPTION:

This container brings a spirit of whimsy and playfulness to the winter garden with stems of juniper, pine, fir, cedar, and spruce placed around a colourful combination of flowering kale and cabbage. The artificial silver stems of fern and the butterfly picks make this a perfect pot for a little girl, or the little girl inside you. My mom liked this container so much that she claimed it as an early Christmas gift!

TIPS AND TRICKS:

- Live plant options for winter combinations are very limited, but the options for accessories are endless: ribbon bows, wired-in Christmas balls, floral picks. You might even decorate this container with Christmas lights.
- Many of my containers are assembled from leftover materials. For this container I looked to the garden and saw a collection of flowering cabbage and kale that could be salvaged. The juniper came from a tree that needed to be removed anyway.
- You can use floral foam in this container instead of potting soil. Either way, keep watering until the soil or floral foam is frozen.

Accessories

Butterfly pick (silver) | ◔◔◔
Fern pick (silver) | ◔◔◔◔◔
Decorative ball (medium) | ◔◔◔◔◔
Decorative ball (large) | ◔◔
Ribbon bow (silver) | ◔

Evergreen boughs
(pine, fir, cedar, spruce)
Filler

Flowering cabbage (white)
Filler | ◔

Juniper stem
Filler/Thriller | ◔◔

Flowering cabbage (purple)
Filler | ◔◔

Flowering kale (purple)
Filler | ◔

Winter

Sterling Silver

SEASON: Winter/Christmas

LIGHT: ☼ ◐ ◑ ●   **WATER:** ◗

DESCRIPTION:

Creating the joyous feeling of Christmas is easy with colours like red, green, and gold. But silver can do the trick too. A pyramid of green is the perfect backdrop for the silver accessories in this container: a collection of various balls, pine cones, ribbon, and floral picks. This eye-catching combo will add a fun and festive air to the holiday season. Although it has a traditional appearance, it would work equally well in a modern home.

TIPS AND TRICKS:

• This gleaming container has instant impact. You may want to continue the theme indoors—for example, decorating your Christmas tree with shiny silver ornaments.
• The pine cones and balls need to be secured to the evergreen boughs with florist wire.
• Water until the soil or floral foam is frozen.

Accessories

Spray pick (silver) | ♦♦♦
Pine cone (silver) | ♦♦♦♦♦♦
Decorative ball (medium silver) | ♦♦♦♦
Decorative ball (large silver) | ♦♦♦
Decorative ball (small silver) | ♦♦♦♦♦♦
Ribbon loop | ♦♦♦

Evergreen boughs
(fir, pine, cedar, spruce)
Filler/Thriller

Northern Star

SEASON: Winter/Christmas

LIGHT: ☼ ☼ ☼ ●   **WATER:** 💧

DESCRIPTION:
Northern Star has a bit of everything I love about the holidays: the scent of conifers, the temptation of the taste of fresh fruit, the comfort of natural pine cones and birch stems, and hope for the future as we wish upon a star. Magnolia stems add colour with their glossy green leaves with an underside of brown, and they will hold up in cold temperatures. This versatile container works in just about any setting, from city to country to cottage.

TIPS AND TRICKS:
- If an item can survive freezing temperatures and add interest, it's a good choice for a winter container. Apples are a great example, but they do have one drawback: raccoons and deer like them as much as you do.
- Magnolia stems are easier to find than they used to be, but you still may have to specially request them from your local florist shop.
- Water until the soil or floral foam is frozen.

Accessories
Decorative ball (bronze) | 🔴🔴🔴
Mesh bow (bronze) | 🔴
Grapevine star | 🔴
Apple ('Granny Smith') | 🔴🔴🔴🔴🔴

Magnolia stems
Filler | 1 bunch

Birch stem
Thriller | 🔴🔴

Sugar pine cone
Accessory | 🔴🔴

Evergreen boughs
(pine, fir, cedar, spruce)
Filler

Bows, Balls, and Stems

SEASON: Winter/Christmas

LIGHT: ○◐◑●   **WATER:** ◐

DESCRIPTION:

Walking through the produce aisle of my local supermarket one day, I saw a crowd of people milling around a display of fruit. The fruit turned out to be pomelo grapefruit, which are huge. I figured if people were drawn to them in the grocery store, they would work in a container. I laid down a bed of evergreens, added bows, balls, and stems, and the result was a simple spherical collection of festive finds.

TIPS AND TRICKS:

- Since the grapefruit are the focal point of this container, they'll work best placed at the front. Any time you use fruit in a container and you're afraid they will roll out, just pick them and stick them. Barbecue skewers will do the trick. Or just take the leftover stems of pine, spruce, or balsam, strip off the needles, and use them as skewers.
- Through careful scientific tests (I put them outside and waited for them to turn black), I determined that pomelo grapefruit will hold up to about −5°C (23°F). On colder nights, bring them indoors.
- Water until the soil or floral foam is frozen.

Accessories

Raffia bow | ◐
Grapevine ball (25 cm/10-inch) | ◐
Pomelo grapefruit | ◐◐

Pine cone (natural)
Accessory | ◐◐◐◐◐◐◐◐

Evergreen boughs
(pine, fir, cedar, spruce)
Filler

Birch stem (silver)
Thriller | ◐◐◐◐◐◐

Winter

First Light

SEASON: Winter/Christmas

LIGHT: ○ ◐ ◑ ●   **WATER:** 💧

DESCRIPTION:
Make your holiday entrance inviting with the warmth of candlelight. A twig wreath on a pot of Christmas greens is a nice spot to nestle a glass hurricane lantern and adds a rustic look to this arrangement. Filling the bottom of the lantern with key limes not only lifts the candle but also adds colour. The base of the lantern is surrounded by a row of oranges, with bronzed grapevine balls added here and there for sparkle. To top it off, a huge bronze mesh bow ties in with the grapevine balls.

TIPS AND TRICKS:
- The twig wreath, fastened to the greens with floral wire, makes a secure spot for the hurricane lantern. The flame of the candle is protected by the glass, but a battery-operated candle would be just as effective.
- A huge bow makes an impressive statement, so don't skimp with the mesh. Fasten the bow to the arrangement with wire.
- The oranges and limes can withstand cool temperatures, but for a more long-lived arrangement that you can reuse each year, you may want to invest in artificial fruit.

Evergreen boughs
(pine, fir, cedar, spruce)
Filler

Accessories

Twig wreath | 🔔
Grapevine ball (bronze) | 🔔🔔🔔🔔🔔🔔
Glass hurricane lantern | 🔔
Pillar candle (white) | 🔔
Mesh bow (bronze) | 🔔
Orange | 🔔🔔🔔🔔🔔🔔🔔🔔🔔🔔
Key limes | 2 bags

Winter

Bloom into Winter

SEASON: Winter/Christmas

LIGHT: ☼◐◑● **WATER:** 💧

DESCRIPTION:
Just because it's Christmas doesn't mean we have to stick to traditional elements. I knew when I saw these dried hydrangeas in early fall that I would find a use for them. When combined with the natural look of moss and the elegance of shiny green decorative balls, this container gives the impression of abundance. The green berry picks at the back give the arrangement height and, of course, it wouldn't be a holiday arrangement without a huge bow.

TIPS AND TRICKS:
- Leave some boughs standing up at the back of the container. This gives the arrangement height and also helps support the hydrangeas. You can separate a larger bloom into smaller florets to place in any empty spots.
- The moss balls are available year round at craft stores and flower shops. Secure them by stabbing them with a wooden skewer and place them at varying heights. The green balls are plastic by the way—glass is just too fragile. Purchase them in various sizes, placing the larger ones at the base of the arrangement, toward the front.
- Add two berry sprays at the back of the arrangement, two more fanning out each side, and the last one dropping down on one side. Balance the arrangement by placing the bow on the opposite side.

Accessories
Decorative ball (lime green) | 🌑🌑🌑🌑
Berry pick (green) | 🌑🌑🌑🌑🌑
Mesh bow (lime green) | 🌑

Hydrangea (dried)
Thriller | 🌑🌑🌑🌑🌑

Moss ball
Accessory | 🌑🌑🌑🌑🌑🌑🌑

Evergreen boughs
(pine, fir, cedar, spruce)
Filler

Feathers and Friends

SEASON: Winter/Christmas

LIGHT: ○◐◑●   **WATER:** 💧

DESCRIPTION:

Red berries and birds are the perfect way to bring nature to your front door, whether at your country retreat or in the city. Natural branches of red berries (use whatever kind you can find at your garden centre or florist shop) fill in the background, while an abundance of Christmas greens spill from this planter. The birdhouse is the centrepiece, accented on one side by two birds under a spray of artificial mistletoe and a big red bow on the other. Another bird among the berries draws the eye up to enjoy their colour. We tested this container at my family's garden centre, and it turned out to be one of the most popular ever. People loved the natural look and the country Christmas feel.

TIPS AND TRICKS:

- Many berries don't last long when the temperature drops, so feel free to use bare branches for height and artificial berry sprays beneath.
- Artificial feathered birds are available throughout the Christmas season in department and craft stores. The birdhouse is anchored to the planter by twigs driven into the base at each corner, and the birds just clip on.

Branches with red berries
Thriller | 5 bunches

Accessories

Artificial bird | 💧💧💧
Birdhouse | 💧
Bird's nest | 💧
Mistletoe (artificial) | 💧
Mesh bow (red) | 💧

Evergreen boughs
(pine, fir, cedar, spruce)
Filler

Winter

Pomegranates and Pine Cones

SEASON: Winter/Christmas

LIGHT: ○◑◐● **WATER:** 💧

DESCRIPTION:

Natural simplicity makes for an elegant planter. An overflowing pot of Christmas evergreens with a bundle of red dogwood stems set in the middle, surrounded by berries, then encircled by pine cones and pomegranates. What could be easier? No showy bow for this arrangement—a few strands of raffia tied in a bow keep the dogwood together and complete the look.

TIPS AND TRICKS:

- Dogwood stems are easy to find during the Christmas season; look for them at florist shops, craft stores, and even supermarkets. For this arrangement, choose stems that are nice and straight.
- The berry stems are available in plastic and look very realistic when combined with the natural pine cones and fruit. Hot-glue or wire floral picks to the pine cones to secure them.
- Poke the pomegranates with a skewer and stick them into floral foam at the base. Pomegranates will survive the whole winter, even if they freeze. You can even dry them and use them year after year. Just bring them indoors, leave them in a dry place, and watch them shrink.

Accessories

Red berry stem (artificial) | 🌰🌰🌰🌰🌰🌰🌰🌰
Pomegranate | 🌰🌰🌰🌰🌰🌰

Evergreen boughs
(pine, fir, cedar, spruce)
Filler

Pine cone (natural)
Accessory | 🌰🌰🌰🌰🌰🌰

Dogwood stems
Thriller | 2 bunches tied with raffia

Winter Reflections

SEASON: Winter/Christmas

LIGHT: ○◐◑●   **WATER:** 💧

DESCRIPTION:

Here's some eye-popping elegance for your Christmas entrance. And no one will guess that it's just your fall Hardy Canadian planter (see page 343) upgraded for the holidays. I placed a bed of Christmas evergreens around the three flowering cabbages and added a silver gazing ball. The assortment of Christmas balls—matte, shiny, and sparkly, in different sizes—pick up the beautiful colours of the cabbage. Topping it all off is a weeping Canadian hemlock to impress your holiday visitors.

TIPS AND TRICKS:

- Here's a great example of how to extend the life of a fall planter. I removed all the plantings from the original except for the hemlock and the flowering cabbage. These can withstand frost—in fact, the cabbage will look even better during the Christmas season and beyond.
- The stems of the evergreens are pushed into the existing soil, so you'll want to do this before the soil freezes. I used pine, balsam and cedar, placing them under and around the cabbage and all around the outside of the pot, leaving the top flat enough to accommodate the gazing ball. The hemlock and cabbage hold the ball in place.
- Choose Christmas balls that pick up the colour of the cabbage and place them randomly around the gazing ball, securing them with skewers glued to the balls and stuck into the soil.
- This planter will need to be watered until freeze-up to keep the hemlock alive. The tree will overwinter in the pot, although it should be kept in a protected spot and watered and fertilized in spring.

Accessories

Decorative ball (medium) | 💧💧💧💧💧💧
Decorative ball (extra large) | 💧
Gazing ball | 💧

Weeping Canadian hemlock
Thriller | 💧

Flowering cabbage (purple)
Filler | 💧💧💧

Evergreen boughs
(pine, fir, cedar, spruce)
Filler

Winter

Acknowledgements

I may be on the cover of *Pot It Up*, but like a fantastic container, this book is a combination of beautiful things—namely, all the people who have supported, guided, and pushed me along the way.

To my best friend and lovely wife, Laurie: thank you for giving me the encouragement to keep going and supporting me as our two boys, Gavin and Matheson, tore up our home (they are only two and four, that's what little boys do!).

Thank you to my mother, Alyce, who lent her creative eye to these plant combinations, made us lunches during the photo shoots, and even allowed us to use the entrance of her home as the backdrop for all the containers.

To my father, Tony, who with his brothers and sisters has built one of Canada's premier garden centres and greenhouse-growing businesses (www.bradfordgreenhouses.com). Dad, thank you for showing me that hard work, determination, and a zest for life can lead to great things.

To my sister, Chiara: thank you for your friendship. Just over 10 years ago, we lost our brother, Tony, to cancer. Today both you and I honour his life by living ours to the fullest.

A big thanks to my family at Citytv, including *BT Toronto* co-hosts Kevin Frankish, Dina Pugliese, and Jenn Valentyne; *CityLine* host Tracy Moore; and friends Tina Cortese, Kevin Forget, and Jamie Haggerty. I'm grateful to you for allowing me to promote the love of gardening to viewers across Canada. To the viewers, listeners, and readers of *BT Toronto*, *CityLine*, *CityNews*, *680News*, *Toronto Sun*, *Canadian Living*, and *Canadian Gardening*: thank you for your love of gardening and passion to get growing!

The experience of writing a book has been exciting, stressful, and emotional but ultimately wonderful because of the team at HarperCollins Canada. Thank you to Kate Cassaday and Brad Wilson, who not only gave me the chance to write but guided the process and kept me on deadline with a gentle but forceful smile. Thanks also to Corey Stewart for her detective work in tracking down all those plant names; to Carolyn Ovell, who continues to be the best PR rep an author could have; to Charidy Johnston for her marketing wizardry; to Alan Jones for the amazing design; and to Kelly Hope for the final touches on the manuscript. To Dan Bortolotti, who helped carve out the flow and really made this book easy to read: you are a talent that needs to be recognized.

I have to recognize also all of my friends and extended family in the horticultural industry who have inspired me and continue to amaze me each day. I can say with confidence that Canadian greenhouse growers are some of the best in the world. A special acknowledgement to Stacey Rumpf and Scott White of Centrade Incorporated, who provided us with all the containers for this book, and to my partner in landscape design, Beth Edney: thank you for your creative accessories. You always know how to improve a pot or a garden. To the Nature Mix team at Premier Tech Home and Garden (Rene, Marie Josée, Bill, and Martin): like great soil, you're always there to nourish. To our assistants Nancy Velso, T.J. Leclair, and Nicoletta Oppedisano: I applaud your hard work, patience, and sweat equity. I hope you can use this experience to grow great careers.

Finally, to my photographer, Shannon J. Ross: two years ago we met as strangers, and today I regard you as one of my best friends. Your talent, your dedication, and your friendship has made *Pot It Up* a dream come true. A book is something to be cherished, and I cherish not only those who have helped me with this book but also all those with whom I've crossed paths along this life of growing opportunities.

Frank Ferragine

How can I possibly fit on one page all of my pride and thanks to all those who helped make this book such a success? Somehow I will try.

When I look back at the two-year journey that has brought this project to fruition, I am truly amazed and inspired by all of the helping hands who lent their time and effort along the way. Without a marvellous team such fruit would surely die on the vine.

First, to Frankie, I would like to thank you most of all for having the vision and creative expertise to make all of these amazing containers come to life. Each and every one of them is a thing of beauty—and not just that, but an achievable masterpiece. You've made sense out of chaos, and I applaud the depth of your creativity in making it all happen. For two years we have worked side by side in all types of conditions to make this book, and you made every working minute fun and worthwhile. Your sense of humour, your unwavering work ethic, and your sense of family and friendship have bolstered us along the way. Thanks a million, my friend!

Also, to Tony and Alyce Ferragine, who gave their time and their home to us to help in all ways that they could. Thank you so much for everything.

To Kate Cassaday, my favourite editor, your intelligence and wisdom have been key components in bringing this project together. I have cherished your insights and clarity tremendously. Your ability to see the big picture and to steer us in all of the right directions has been invaluable, and I know the success of this book will in no small part be due to you. I have gained valuable experience from having had the good fortune to work with you and the rest of the team at HarperCollins.

To my wife, Robyn, who has supported me with insights and ideas along the way, your good taste and stylish sense have mixed wonderfully into the project. I feel blessed to have you by my side. And to my family and friends who build me up and yet keep me grounded, thanks for always being a real and true compass.

Finally, to you the reader, please accept my humblest and most ardent thanks for reading our book. May it inspire you and help you to achieve marvellous things in and around your home. It required countless hours and many hands to create, and now it is up to you to fill the world with your own creative containers. Thanks everyone!

Shannon J. Ross

Pot It Up

Index

Index

Index